*Jungian Reflections on
Literary and Film Classics:
opus 2*

Legends of the Fall

*Jungian Reflections on
Literary and Film Classics:
opus 2*

Legends of the Fall

by
Richard Chachere

CYPREMORT POINT PRESS
Lafayette, Louisiana 70505

COPYRIGHT © 2004 BY RICHARD CHACHERE
ALL RIGHTS RESERVED

No part of this book may be used or reproduced in any manner whatsoever without written permission from the Publisher, except in the case of brief quotations embodied in critical articles and reviews.

Library of Congress Cataloging-in-Publication data
Chachere, Richard
Jungian Reflections on Literary and Film Classics, Opus 2, Legends of the Fall
p. cm.
ISBN 0-9740482-1-6

FIRST PRINTING
About the Cover: Near the top of the cover is a drawing of the Hopi Indian "Spirit Bear." It is symbolic of the alchemists' quest for gold—the transformed berserker (bear.) By happy coincidence, this Spirit Bear is also the author's logo.

Book design by Mark R. Bacon
Author photo (back cover) by Terri Fensel
Printed in the United States of America on acid-free paper.

Published by Cypremort Point Press
P.O. Box 51705
Lafayette, Louisiana 70505

Dedication

Dedicated to the memory of my father, Joe Chachere—
my "Colonel"—whose hatred of his childhood poverty,
and whose exquisite hard work
provided the means for my own "legends."

"There is deep doctrine in the legend of the fall:
it is the expression of a dim presentiment that the
emancipation of ego-consciousness was a Luciferian deed."

>   Jung's essay, *Theriomorphic Symbolism in Fairy Tales*,
>   CW 9i, paragraph 420

Table of Contents

Cast and Credits	xiii
Acknowledgements	xv
Foreword	xvii
Prelude	xxiii
1. Legends of the Fall	1
2. Fathers and Sons	19
3. Love and Jealousy	39
4. Tristan, a Knight's Tale	59
5. The Confrontation with the Unconscious	81
6. Reflections on Evil	103
7. Dealing with One's Bear	133
8. Postlude: A Tale of Two Colonels	145
Glossary	149
Bibliography	153
Index	157
About the Author	166

Theatrical Release in 1994

Director: Edward Zwick
Producers: William Wittliff, Edward Zwick & Marshall Herskovitz
Author: Jim Harrison
Screenwriters: Susan Shilliday & William Wittliff
Cinematographer: John Toll
Composer: James Horner
Editor: Steven Rosenblum

Cast:

Tristan Ludlow	Brad Pitt
Col. William Ludlow	Anthony Hopkins
Alfred Ludlow	Aidan Quinn
Susannah Fincannon Ludlow	Julia Ormond
Samuel Ludlow	Henry Thomas
Isabel Two	Karina Lombard
One Stab	Gordon Tootoosis
Isabel Ludlow	Christina Pickles
Decker	Paul Desmond
Pet	Tantoo Cardinal

⚜ ⚜ ⚜ ⚜ ⚜ ⚜ ⚜ ⚜

Acknowledgements

Obviously, in a work of this nature, support came from many directions. Once again, I give thanks to my seminal group, the Acadiana Friends of Jung who encouraged the lecture series and then enthusiastically, the book.

Upon first seeing the movie, I was thunderstruck by the story and knew immediately I had to do "work" on this, enmeshed as I was at the time in an "affair of the heart." Susannah's fate was especially poignant to me. So was Alfred's look when he walked in on Tristan and Susannah. It is a look I have never forgotten.

But like the desolate scene in the movie after Tristan's leaving and the Colonel's stroke, dust gathered on my resolve to do a lecture series on it, until the feminine moved and several women voted for "*Legends*" in the company of Dostoevsky, Hemingway and Tolstoy. I remember Sarah Mills as being especially verbal and that my own Susan reminded me that this sound track was her favorite of all. So I thank you, ladies of the Acadiana Friends of Jung.

Thanks go to Rebecca Mills, my secretary; to Mary Beth Comeaux of the AFJ; and especially to Sandra Walker, who arduously transcribed the lecture notes; as well as to Lou Daleen, who did a yeoman's work in editing those myriad notes and trying to bring them into manageable form.

This work would not have happened without the amazing energy and devotion of Geraldine Hubbell. To her I owe a great deal of gratitude, as over and over again, she tried to keep the ship sailing, not to mention her amazing speed typing and correcting.

Thanks also to Mark Bacon, the art director for the book, and to my many clients whose dreams and stories enrich the material. Especially again, is the creative wellspring that the Acadiana Friends of Jung were for me, and for their interest, support and questions…that is a whole other story.

In addition, in this man's tale, I want to thank the four men who particularly aided me: Bill Atkinson from London, who insisted over and over that I get this in print—always with a positive Aikido thrust; Ian Player, whose emails from South Africa were synchronistically amazing, always at the right time, with just the right word of support; George Wagner, ally and comrade, fellow admirer of Laurens van der Post and Joseph Henderson, to whom I owe so much for these connections, and more.

And finally, my new friend and colleague, Theo Abt, who arrived in my life at a crucial time for "Legends." His support is already "of legends." I feel as though all four of these men have been "colonels" to me.

And, of course, my dear Susan, who carries the feminine in the way Susannah had hoped.

Foreward

When Richard Chachere asked me to write a foreword to this book, I had no idea that doing so would reconnect me to one of the most weird experiences of my life: a midnight encounter with a bear on a mountain ridge, close to a forest fire. Nor did I know that it would revive the painful memory of my father's involvement in the First World War. But more of that later.

The movie *Legends of the Fall*, based on Jim Harrison's novella, was released in 1994. For some reason it passed me by—I have been unaware of it for the last ten years. When the film first appeared, I had only just retired from work and I suppose other concerns filled my life.

I came to the movie only recently, and I found it deeply affecting. On a personal level it evoked the bear confrontation, the forest fire and the War. In its tangled and tragic love involvements there are faint echoes of the *Tristan and Isolde* myth, even to the names and origin of its main characters. Terrible things happen. There is splendor in the Montana wilderness; devastation in the killing fields of France—both made vivid by superb cinematography. The casting is inspired, the portrayals accomplished and intelligent. The music penetrates the heart. And pervading the entire story is the compelling spirit of the Bear, in its natural and symbolic forms.

Chachere has called the film a great masterpiece and in this book he tells us why. Skillfully he reveals the deeper meanings within the story, and makes them relevant to our lives.

In essence, the film is about a family in the waning Old West. The father, Colonel William Ludlow, appalled by the carnage of the Indian Wars, renounces combat and leaves the Army to establish a ranch in the foothills of the Montana Rockies.

One day his wife departs for the East, fearing the winter, fearing bears. Mysteriously, she never returns, leaving her husband to raise their three sons.

The eldest is Alfred: sensible, assured in business and politics. He follows the rules. The youngest, Samuel, is idealistic, impulsive and quite impervious to the demands of relationships. Tristan is the middle son, his father's favorite, daring, questing through labyrinths of the soul, and connected from birth with the spirit of the Bear.

Samuel returns to the ranch from college with his fiancée, the lovely Susannah. She sends a "frisson" through the men. Samuel is agog with the rights and wrongs of the First World War; he declares his intent to go to Europe and fight for England, causing anger to his father, who detests warfare. His declaration shocks Susannah. Evidently Samuel knows nothing of the reality expressed by the writer Robertson Davies: after we link our destiny to someone, we neglect that person at our peril.

Yet one feels sympathy for Samuel. He is unseasoned, caught in the archetypal conflict between youth's call to adventure and the duties of commitment. He is like Pagnol's young Marius on the waterfront of Marseilles, torn between sea-fever and his love for the fish-stall worker, Fanny.

So the Colonel's family is fractured. All three sons go to war, Tristan charged by his father to protect Samuel. But Samuel is killed, Tristan goes berserk, and the wheel of pain and tragedy turns.

The narrator of the story is a Native American, One Stab, servant-companion to the Colonel, and a kind of "godfather" to Tristan. One Stab's voice and presence arch over the events and other players.

Richard Chachere's masterly analysis of these characters and events, and his reflections on their significance, delineate the mythic dimensions of the story, enticing a viewing of the film again and again. Here I shall mention just a few aspects of the movie, which particularly struck me.

The first is the early scene where the Colonel, a Cavalry officer, vehemently expresses to his disgust for war. He draws his sword, throws the unsheathed weapon into the earth, and walks away.

In the military realm the sword signifies strength and courage; it is a symbol of the highest martial virtue. That gesture of disdain for it shows clearly the Colonel's surrender to conscience. It is an image of absolute renunciation.

Yet ironically it is not, finally, absolute. At the close, old and decrepit, huddled in a great bearskin coat, the Colonel is compelled to take up arms again. He resorts to the gun, and, true to the way of the warrior, brings death once more. It is a manifestation of Shakespeare's words, "There is a divinity that shapes our ends/Rough-hew them how we will." (*Hamlet*, Act 5, sc. 2, ll. 10-11)

Then there are the women: the enigmatic departure of Isabel One, the Colonel's wife, and the arrival years later of Susannah, Samuel's fiancée. The going and coming of the feminine change the dynamics of the situation, each creating its own disorder.

Shortly after Susannah's arrival there is an interesting exchange between her and Isabel Two, daughter of Decker and Pet, the ranch hands. Isabel Two, aged only thirteen, declares that she will marry Tristan—a statement of remarkable prescience. I was startled by the scene, because I remembered that in 1850 another Isabel had accurately predicted her own marriage. This was Isabel Arundell. Walking along the ramparts of Boulogne with her younger sister, she saw a man who astounded her. Isabel, then nineteen, later wrote, "I was completely magnetized, and when he had got a little distance away I turned to my sister and whispered to her, 'That man will marry me'."

That man was the British explorer, Sir Richard Burton. Anyone who has seen Sir Frederick Leighton's portrait of Burton, showing the wound of the spear driven through his face, will understand why Isabel Arundell was smitten.

As for Susannah, she carries a doom-seed. There is Samuel's betrayal of her by going off to war; her tragic intertwinings with the three brothers; Tristan's flight, and her impossible promise to him to "wait forever," echoing his own impossible promise to protect Samuel in the trenches. And finally there is her season in hell, through what Richard Chachere calls the betrayal of her own heart, her marriage to Alfred, culminating in her suicide after an appalling confession to Tristan.

Central to the film, as to the Colonel's family, is Tristan. He is "the rock on which many were broken," yet he is broken himself by his failure to save Samuel in the War.

The desperate ride to rescue his brother, his fall from the horse in bullets and flame, his charge through mud and slaughter only to see Samuel tangled and shot in the barbed wire—these are scenes which chill the blood. I find them almost unbearable, because shortly before my own father died I asked him about his experience of that War. He began to speak about a battle at the Dardanelles, when he was twenty, before he went to the trenches. While his unit was crossing to the Turkish shore on a raft, machine guns from the cliffs swept men and horses into the sea. He was among the roughly ten per cent who survived that crossing. He broke down as the memory revived, and said no more.

Tristan sees his brother die in the barbed wire, and he goes berserk, killing wildly. Only Julian Grenfell's line from "Into Battle" can illustrate that madness—a madness seen also in the Colonel's face as he fires his gun at the end:

> And when the burning moment breaks,
>   And all things else are out of mind,
> And only joy of battle takes
>   Him by the throat, and makes him blind,
> Through and blindness he shall know,
>   Not caring much to know, that still
> Nor lead nor steel shall reach him, so
>   That it be not the Destined Will.

Tristan is discharged from the Army, but he does not go home. He goes to sea instead, because there is a need for recovery. He craves a cleansing from the inner detritus of war. As Richard Chachere observes, Sir Lauren van der Post experienced this after World War II and his involvement in the post-war turmoil of South-East Asia. In his case he camped by the Pafuri River, and it was the bushveld and animals of Africa which purged his spirit.

Eventually restored, Tristan comes home to the ranch, and to Susannah. Their love, though, is ill fated. The trauma of Samuel's death is reactivated by a calf hopelessly enmeshed in barbed wire. Tristan shoots it—he becomes distant, detached from reality. He leaves the ranch again, fleeing into a "dark night of the soul," reminiscent of Jung's own period of near-psychosis. He is in the grip of the Bear. Richard Chachere guides us through that dark night to Tristan's ensuing return and transformation. The way he guides us is a mark of his unique talent because it is an uplifting experience for the reader.

I mentioned earlier my personal experience with a bear. The story, I feel, is worth telling because of the synchronicities involved with this film, which concerns the power and spirit of the Bear. First, the chances are small that the person asked to write this Foreword would himself have had an encounter with that animal. And it is a million to one that the same person would have got into that encounter through one of the words in the film's title: the Fall.

I often visit the Southwestern United States, and in the summer of 1996 I found myself in Santa Fe, New Mexico, which has a fine Aikido dojo. The ability to fall safely from a throw is essential, and although I could do the standard rolls, in those days I had difficulty with "high falls," where one is flipped over some 225 degrees. In Santa Fe, I practiced these so hard that I tore a stomach muscle. Mortified, I withdrew from training to go hiking.

Mount Atalaya is nearby, so with tent and provisions I trudged up to its 9,000 foot summit ridge for a couple of nights' camping. I put up the tent, and enjoyed the vista of both valleys: Santa Fe to the south and a forest to the north.

Around mid-afternoon I noticed smoke above the trees, spreading slowly. It was a forest fire. Exhausted by the climb, the last thing I wanted was to decamp, so I considered my options. There seemed no immediate danger unless the fires flared; what I feared was engulfment by the fire in the night. I located escape routes to the south, and decided to stay. I set the alarm to wake me every hour to check on the fire. And I hoped that the storm clouds over Santa Fe, approaching the ridge, would break over the fire and dampen it. That happened, so I went to sleep tired but relaxed.

The noise that woke me was quite near: a deep, coughing bark, clearly from a big animal. In the instant of waking I experienced an intense white light in my head, and the fiercest rage I have ever known. Spontaneously I duplicated the sound. I turned over—feeling no fear whatever. The bark was repeated twice, each time from a greater distance. I went back to sleep.

Next morning I found no tracks, but I knew the animal was a bear, probably escaping the fire. I was bemused by my own reaction; throwing back to the bear its own challenge—if challenge it was. And I was thankful for my practice of Ki-ais in Aikido.

I have never known what to make of that experience. Seeing *Legends of the Fall* vividly revived it, because the Bear dominates the film.

C.G. Jung, given the totem name of Bear by the Pueblo Indians, was a great man with a formidable intellect. His concepts, however, are so profound that they are often hard to understand, especially in translation. Many of his ideas seem elusive. Richard Chachere's great gift is an ability to take these ideas and concepts, identify their workings in life, literature and art, and present them in a way we can all understand and appreciate. In doing that he provides a most valuable service to society.

Tristan's own relationship with the Bear, actual and symbolic, is one of the most haunting aspects of the film. It is what carries one into the myth. Swaddled in bearskin as a baby, initiated by combat with a bear in youth, possessed by the Bear in his dark night of the soul, transformed and redeemed by its power in mid-life, Tristan finally finds death by it in the forest.

In a strange way his end reminds me of the death of Conrad's *Lord Jim*—also in a forest, also apparently sought with conscious intent. To each, I feel, his death was an opportunity. As Conrad puts it:

> And that's the end. He passes away under a cloud, inscrutable at heart, forgotten, unforgiven, and excessively romantic. Not in the wildest days of his boyish visions could he have seen the alluring shape of such an extraordinary success! For it may very well be that in the short moment of his last proud unflinching glance, he had beheld the fact of that opportunity."

And as One Stab says of Tristan: "It was a good death."

This story is an epic. Richard Chachere matches that quality in his telling of it.

—William Atkinson
London, England

Prelude

This book, *Legends of the Fall,* like my *Opus I, American Beauty,* is the result of lectures given over a period of months to the Acadiana Friends of Jung in Lafayette, Louisiana. Here we have tried to keep the original lively form of a more "give and take" format. Hopefully, the transition from the spoken to the written word will not be noticeable.

This is a book about a movie so it would be beneficial to familiarize yourself with the movie. You may want to purchase your own copy because the references to scenes are too frequent and important to be able to assimilate from only one viewing of *Legends*.

In the film, the musical score is memorable and epically haunting. Purchasing the CD might be a requisite as well. Typically, the lectures began with a musical meditation in order to set a tone. I would encourage a reading in that same spirit. That way, more of the whole person is engaged, rather than just the head. One knows from Jung, that "just the head" won't do.

Let me give a deep, heartfelt thanks to Jim Harrison, the creator/writer of *Legends of the Fall,* to actor Jack Nicholson who made it possible; and to the creators of the film, Edward Zwick and James Horner, who captured its spirit. Finally, thanks to the filmmakers, the screenwriters and all who gave us this great masterpiece.

Why do I call it a great masterpiece? Precisely because of its title: it touches us on a mystic level. If a modern person ever allows himself to go to the level beyond intellect, beyond "how it should be," beyond books and theories, he will reach the level of "felt experience." The modern reader/viewer/listener must suspend this "critical apparatus." Chances are, the more degrees and the more sophistication a person has, the more suspending he or she will have to do. He/she should allow himself 'to drop down' into a receptive place to allow himself to go with the flow of the story. The more resistance one experiences, the more one can know how much he or she may need to go against to get to that receptive place. It is not easy for us moderns. It is not easy for a Cajun from Louisiana, for example, to transplant himself visually or emotionally to Montana. Neither can a native New Yorker. But if the Louisianian or New Yorker can allow the archetypal level a chance, he might be surprised at how quickly he has been "transported."

That is the magic of myth and legend, which transports a person. We do not transport ourselves. It is something that happens to us— we live a myth. We do not create a myth. We are either in it or not.

The trick is to know that. The further trick available only to us moderns is the trick of consciousness, to know what one is experiencing. Furthermore, as Jung elucidated brilliantly and experientially, we would be able to relate to what one experiences rather than having to live it out blindly. We all know this. We know the difference between going to a party and having a great time, versus going to a party and "becoming the party!" The difference between taking care of grandmother versus going to see grandmother and feeling for her so much one becomes identified with her age or loneliness or illness is that one leaves a visit drained and exhausted. And one wonders why one dreads visiting grandmother next time.

In the first case, one is clear—conscious—of what one is doing, but does not identify with it (e.g., an errand of mercy.) In the other, one identifies with the errand of mercy and gets "possessed" by it.

These are two very different ways of approaching the same event/issue, but they make a world of difference psychologically.

The first gives meaning. The second drains life and energy, and the ego is in the wrong place. Instead of being a gracious servant, it leaves one irritated and feeling taken advantage of.

The trick with myth and legend is to learn from them, be moved by them, and to experience them (be touched by) but not to identify with them in the sense of wanting "to live them out."

For example, one can be moved by the Colonel's "hatred of war" without having to literally move. One can want "to get to the other side of the mountains" without having to give up one's present job.

Jung shows us that myth and legend need to be taken symbolically. That means taking things on an inner metaphorical level. In this example "to go to the other side of the mountains" could mean to change one's attitude about the busyness in one's life. It could mean to learn to live the symbolic life in New York City. A person could have a quiet corner in one's apartment "to get away from it all."

Which is what moderns do with extravagant vacations—we keep re-inventing exotic travel places "to go here and go there"—when all along it is really about "getting away from it all." But we can go from New York City to India, the most introverted opposite country in the world, and bring "it all" with us. It is not about "out there." It is not about "going." For some physically bound people that going may help, but this journey is really about an inner journey of turning within in one's imagination and letting the whole busy world drop away.

—Richard Chachere

1

Legends of the Fall

Track 1,
Overture

Legends of the Fall is a movie to be watched with the heart while letting one's spirit soar. The film touches on epic themes and on *"legends"*—legends in the sense of things that are remembered. It is important then, to watch the movie as well as to listen to the majestic score. I suggest that you rent or buy the video because we will try to coordinate the chapters with certain scenes of the movie.

Right from the beginning, it is important to watch and listen, not with one's critical faculties as much as with one's feeling of wanting to "experience the experience," letting the movie speak directly to one's feelings.

In that sense, we will not be speaking intellectually. Instead, we are going to a different place. We will let the movie speak for itself while we do active listening, as opposed to passive listening—"just sitting there." We will notice and *reflect* on what occurs to us as we watch the movie. That is *active listening*.

The movie is based, faithfully and extraordinarily, on the small novella by Jim Harrison. It would be helpful to read Harrison's novella even though the material in this book is based primarily on the film. Unfortunately, Harrison's book did not come to attention until after the film. By comparison with the film, the novella comes off as rather "austere" and laconic. Nowhere is it as lush or as beautiful as the film. But of course, those qualities are possible in a movie with an Academy Award winning photographer like John Toll. The film was directed by Edward Zwick, who did an extraordinary job. Zwick mentioned the feeling of awe he experienced upon his first reading of *"Legends of the Fall."* That awe comes through in the film. The musical score captured by James Horner also conveys the same majesty, so for that reason the music is used throughout our presentation as a meditative background. (The treble staff icon with suggestions for listening from the CD soundtrack will help to guide you along the way; see page one.)

One of the qualities one might notice immediately about the soundtrack is that it is unabashedly uplifting and inspiring. Despite all the love and loss, all the death and tragedy, the music soars at appropriate times. Yet in "Samuel's Death" (track 5) and "Farewell/Descent into Madness" (Track 7) and "Revenge" (track 11), the music can plummet to the depths in a most chilling way.

James Horner has done a masterful job of distilling (a word that alchemists loved) all these emotions into a profound musical score that can haunt one for decades. *Legends* will forever have his sound. At the same time it is evocative and "goose-pimply" in all the right moments with a musical palette as rich as any of Monet's. It does so with lush, unabashed feeling. It seems to me an honoring of the feminine in a remarkable way, for surely music and feeling and emotion are associated with the eternal feminine. This may be why some men and/or thinking types had trouble with this film.

Kudos to Horner for giving us such a rich gift that forever enshrines something it seems that we need in our culture—real soul and the "inner life" of this film (to quote Ed Zwick, the director, in the soundtrack notes.) An inner life that is not only in touch with the feminine and real feeling, but one which honors it.

This movie is about the substance of "legends," of myth, and it is filmed that way.

✤ ✤ ✤ ✤ ✤ ✤ ✤ ✤ ✤

One Stab: "Some people hear their own inner voices with great clearness and they live by what they hear. Such people become crazy or they become legends."

So begins a great saga of the West, a saga close to the psyche of many of us. Right from One Stab's opening lines, we know that we are going on an interesting, gripping journey—one that promises to be different, that will focus on *inner dynamics*, "strange" for the language of Hollywood.

Why? Because of One Stab's words "Some people hear their own inner voices with great clearness." Because it focuses on inner voices, rather than outer. Those inner voices are memorable and significant words. Those are also scary words. We are told something extremely frightening in terms of our ordinary consciousness, something that is usually associated with craziness—people who listen to inner voices. One Stab quickly adds these words—"such people become crazy" or "they become legends." He adds the proviso "or." One either listens to those voices without discrimination and one becomes crazy, or one has the chance through consciousness to become a "legend." That is going to be the story of Tristan.

✣ ✣ ✣ ✣ ✣ ✣ ✣ ✣

The beginning sets the stage. The Narrator is One Stab, an elder of the Cree nation, who tells us the story of the Ludlow family of Montana. He tells us that Colonel Ludlow had three sons, and that Tristan was his favorite. He tells us also of the special bond, or connection, between One Stab and Tristan:

"As he grew into a man, I taught him the great joy of the kill— when a hunter cuts out its warm heart and holds it in his hands, setting its spirit free. Colonel Ludlow had three sons, but Tristan was his favorite. I had had sons too. They were gone now, forever. It was a very bad time. The Colonel had tried to help the people. But it was no use. So he decided to go his own way. He wanted to "lose the madness over the mountains," he said, "and begin again." "Lose the madness," he said. And so we lived for many years, and the boys grew strong."

Do you have a sense of the mythic dimension of this story already? Beyond the title, which gives us that mythic intimation right from the start, there is also scenery and the music. The whole production is very lush, beautiful, and romantic. It can waft one away. The main characters of the story are the Colonel, played by Anthony Hopkins, Tristan, played by Brad Pitt, Susannah, played by Julia Ormond and Alfred, played by Aidan Quinn. That quartet of actors should be enough to captivate most of us already, and the acting is wonderful. Then there is the cinematography: the beautiful scenery of the mountains in the background with the soaring music to match give one a sense of transcendence. Transcendence means "out of the ordinary." It lifts you above things.

A swamplander from Lafayette, Louisiana can tell what it means to go out West to the mountains, because after one has been in the swamp a long time, one loses perspective, and can't see "nothin' but crawfish and sugarcane." Out West are wide-open spaces and huge vistas, and the geography affects the psyche—it can give one perspective again. The cinematographer John Toll offers us that perspective in these beautiful opening scenes as we approach a myth we are all familiar with—*The Fall*. Here is a Western Garden of Eden. But it is also the perspective of the West and of the Western—a great archetype for Americans.

The Colonel is a remarkable man because he "gets it right"—he knows the terrible toll that separation from Nature has on the psyche of man, "The Fall," and he "goes to the other side of the mountain to lose the madness." (One interpretation of the Fall is that it occurred when we separated ourselves from Nature.) Here, the Colonel's rejection of civilization and all its ills represents an attempt to return to Nature, to undo at least for himself and his family, the harm that the separation caused. Tristan is the only one of his sons who understands this. He immerses himself in the world of One Stab and the Bear. These are beautiful scenes. It is very important to know that Tristan was his father's favorite, because of this connection. Besides Tristan, the first person noticed, as we've said, is the Colonel—Colonel Ludlow, played by Anthony Hopkins. The Colonel is also an unusual man. He loved the American Indians when it was not fashionable to love them, in the mid-to-late nineteenth century. Although he was a colonel in the military, he hated war. That still is certainly not fashionable or ordinary.

The wonderful thing about psychology as Jung understood it is the ability to take the psyche, to hold it at a distance and to observe it, as if under a microscope. Psychology is at its best when we look at the psyche as a living thing, and as a source of wisdom. To understand what the psyche is getting at, we observe, "What is getting *me*?" One way is to notice what grabs us when we go to a movie or to the theater. Before we go further, let us comment about the importance of movies, or theater and plays and screenplays, to psychology as Jung understood it.

The Greeks used the verb "to play"—the same word—for both the theater and for athletic events. Both involve a person in the play of the psyche, the play of the soul. It is a way to learn about oneself. Marie-Louise von Franz, in her wonderful film series, *The Way of the Dream*, tells us that there is an archetypal background to human living that may be discovered in the myths and fairy tales coming down to us from the past. Fairy tales are particularly important, as von Franz has demonstrated in her work, because they contain the myths necessary for our orientation to life. This is why fairy tales are important to us and why parents should read or tell them to their children. Do not buy into the fashionable bias that fairy tales are too violent, too brutal, or too destructive, because they are not. Fairy tales can be healing sources of life. And in that sense, very real and just right.

Here is an example: In European fairy tales, there is the widespread motif of the princess locked up in a tower. In one of the most well-known, a witch imprisons the princess, Rapunzel. It is the Mother figure behind the scenes (the witch) who brings forth the constellation of life. When Rapunzel is imprisoned, the lovers cannot meet on earth. Only when Rapunzel comes down to earth from her tower, and after the prince has wandered in pain and misery long enough, do they finally meet. Contrary to popular belief, that tale is not just a weird story from 1700. These scenes happen today in modern relationships. In *Legends of the Fall*, we will notice how the mother's presence behind the scenes in the Ludlow family has an effect as well. Could she be the "Eve of Eden" here?

Dr. von Franz goes on to say that in our own time, movies may touch many of these psychological facts, and some movies may replace the telling of fairy tales and myths of former times. But a word of caution is in order, because not all movies touch the inner archetypal world. Few films tell stories that touch us on this level at all. The films that do are often attractive to the public because we really do need myths. This can be proved by the film's popularity.

We need these myths because they provide orientation to life, and because they provide us a map of the dream world of the unconscious. We need them whether we know it or not, or whether we believe it or not.

Therefore, pay attention to your reactions and to what touches you. Pay attention to those with whom you identify in this film. In *Transformation of the Libido,* Edward Edinger writes:

> We have great opportunities for increasing our self-knowledge by noticing what it is we identify with, and the theater is a wonderful opportunity to make those observations. People do not all identify with the same things by any means, and the particular dramatic events that most move some people can leave others cold, because different complexes are struck. I urge you to take this remark of Jung's very seriously. We are barraged with dramatic images everywhere, not only on the stage, but in the movies and television. Whenever we note what particular theme or dramatic event moves us, we are collecting a part of our own dispersed psyche. Our psyche does not start on the inside. Our psyche begins in identification with the world, with the environment; it is spread everywhere. The theater offers us a chance to notice what it is we respond to. If we are psychologically motivated, we can recognize this as a piece of our own psyche and withdraw the projection. Then it is no longer a quality of the play, but it belongs to oneself. (1994, pp.5-6)

To begin with, your psyche is "out there," all over the place. The more "out there" you are, the more your psyche is "out there" as well. That is why some of us find it very hard to get in touch with ourselves—the soul is inaccessible because it is not here. It's "out there." Life works very hard to get us "in here." All the great religions are about that process and so is life itself, according to Jung.

The psyche can be "out there" in a woman, or in the neighborhood, or in the job, or in God knows what. As silly as it may seem, and as shy as it may make us feel, it is important to notice what draws us. It is important to notice your feelings about Tristan, or Susannah or Alfred as we watch this film. It is important to notice what he or she does for you. Then it will no longer be just a quality of the movie, or of the actors. It will belong to you.

✠ ✠ ✠ ✠ ✠ ✠ ✠ ✠ ✠

What does it mean that the Colonel's favorite son is named Tristan? His name comes from one of the greatest love stories of all time—*Tristan and Isolde*. Perhaps coincidentally, (or perhaps not) his mother's name is Isabel (not a far reach from Isolde) and Tristan marries the younger Isabel Two.

If you are familiar with the myth of *Tristan and Isolde,* you know that it is tragic. You know that it is about romantic love. Then you can be made immediately aware of the archetypal background and mythic quality of this story. Then perhaps you can understand how the title—*Legends of the Fall*—the cinematography, and the music all appropriately reflect that mythical, archetypal background. There is much more to this story than what appears on the surface.

The narrator, One Stab, tells us that Tristan was born in a very difficult time, in "the moon of the falling leaves" before "a terrible winter," and that his mother almost lost her life in childbirth. The Colonel brought the infant to One Stab, who wrapped the baby in a bearskin, and held him all night long. Tristan had an unusual birth, already the mark of an auspicious man. Tristan's first encounter with life was with a bear, and he was wrapped in a bearskin. In olden times in Germany, the followers of Wotan (god of war and head of the gods) in Wagner's *Ring* cycle, wore bearskins. The word "berserk" comes from that tradition. The bear became "his" animal throughout his life. As you begin to notice that, to feel that, to associate all that a bear really is, to recall our expression "to bare all" or "to go berserk" as Tristan does often in the story, then the bear as a symbol becomes very fascinating. One Stab tells us that Tristan was spoken to by "the bear inside him." We notice that the bear is expressed in Tristan's anger and aggression and rage, and that his bear-qualities are lived in the film. (We will see that "our own bears" have to be faced and dealt with, or they will eat us. We will see then that it is a modern problem, and very important.) Symbolically, the bear is livid with anger, with aggression, and with rage. Paradoxically, he also can be a symbol of great courage. One could say the bear here is a great alchemical symbol; he will have to be tended by Tristan as his "prima materia."

Aggression taken to its collective extreme is war, and it is the Colonel's disgust with war and his love of the beauty of nature that sets the whole film in motion. All three sons go to war over his objections. All three sons are scarred by the war. One son is killed in the war, and the family is never the same. There are many things about family life in this film, and not all of them are romantic.

We noticed that it is the Colonel's disgust with war that sets the whole film in motion. Perhaps a psychological digression is in order here. To go to the other side of the mountains—to get ready—often as one gets older, one feels the need "to go to the other side." Symbolically, it is what Jung expressed by the change of energies after mid-life. Then, especially, one will experience the need to "get away" from the extreme aggression of modern life. Colonel Ludlow expresses this brilliantly. In that sense, he becomes a model for all of us—of going "to the other side"—the unconscious of which Jung spoke.

Shockingly, he embraces his enemies, the Indians.

Next, he leaves the military, even though he is a military man.

Then, he goes away "to the other side." He is going to listen to other energies, other voices.

It is also important to note that the Colonel, after a life of fighting, turns his back on the violence of war. The aggression of that intensity we spoke of. There comes a time for all of us when the life of intensity, of intense combat and conflict must be given up lest it burn us all out. It is in this sense that one can speak of Colonel Ludlow as a wisdom-figure here. He "gets" it right. He is also right about the evil of war.

But notice, his choice does not protect his sons.

Furthermore, it even does not protect him.

We have noticed already that a parent cannot pass his experience on to his children—they have to learn it the "old-fashioned-way." There is also the irony that war plays here. The Colonel goes to the "other side of the mountains" to get away from war, and all three of his sons wind up going across the mountains to encounter war.

Here is another psychological corollary: you cannot, by edict, keep something out. You cannot order something not to happen. In fact, the more absolute you are in your condemnation, the more you ensure that it will happen and that it will be brought up. Jung would say, "It constellates activities."

It is almost as if the Colonel's opposition to war constellates his sons' interest in war. This happens in families. If parents are too one-sided about an issue, you can be sure the children will bring that issue up in the way they live.

In the movie, this is the last line describing Tristan: "Always alone, always apart, somehow solitary. Tristan is buried in Canada."

How would Jung describe that? He would describe Tristan as the unique personality. Pointing this out may make the critics understand why this movie created such a stir, and why the ladies responded so intensely to the character Brad Pitt played. It is fair to say that something in us wants to honor that individuated personality in us. That may seem a bit heavy, but it just might carry weight. For that reason, this movie takes us into deep, wonderful water.

Many women really loved this film. In fact, a vote from women who attended the original lectures led to the work on this book. But one wonders why women would love such a terrible story! Everybody gets wretched. The family is wracked by every imaginable assault upon it. Everybody gets eaten. One might ask, "What is so romantic about it?"

One possible answer is that in *Legends,* life is *lived*—life is lived, connected and stirred, and it is red-blooded. It is a "hell of a story." This movie is full of life and Eros. Women and the feminine have a great stake in Eros and relatedness. As Jack Sanford, the Jungian analyst, often said, women can take almost anything if Eros is present—almost anything. The greatest tribute to the feminine is that she loves life in this sense.

However, the critics were in stark contrast to the opinions of all the women and men who loved this movie. This author could not find *one* positive review. So what does one do when he experiences something this important which the critics are trashing? How does one tell actual insight from destructive criticism? Poisonous criticism often drips with sarcasm, which never comes from the center. Sarcasm is never helpful. The intention of sarcasm is to render one inferior; real insight does not make one feel inferior. Real insight makes one feel equal to the task, interested, and curious and usually it is helpful. Von Franz's favorite remark about critics was, "People who write letters to the editor, or newspapers, would do better to go to their journals first and work out their complexes, and then see if they have anything left to say." Most of us struggle to keep our heads above water and to trust our own "feeling reactions," so we need to be aware of poisonous criticism, from whatever source. We are not talking about opinions, of who is right or who is wrong, or of competence or the lack of it. We are talking about honoring what touches us. It is a matter of feeling and not letting criticism rob you of your "feeling value." Feeling can be quite sensitive; it is the best sense.

It is also a matter of valuing. The intellect can be cold and logical—that is its genius. But there are other values. For instance: "I see this scene that moves me." This is using "feel" in Jung's sense of "the feeling function," the function of valuing. This is a very important distinction, one that goes to the heart of Jungian psychology and Jung's genius.

For example, that is why we can have the dichotomy of the scientist who is correct with his facts and still draws the wrong human conclusion, or the brilliant doctor, (not coincidentally, Dr. Jekyll & Mr. Hyde, a healer and a killer), who is a terrible person. The recent play *Copenhagen* is also a great metaphor for this. The play is a brilliant exposition of the difficulty of values when two noted nuclear physicists debate their work—one for the Nazis, one for America—and the portrayal of how close the opposites of good and evil really can be.

⚜ ⚜ ⚜ ⚜ ⚜ ⚜ ⚜ ⚜ ⚜

The opening lines in the film set the mark. The Colonel could not stand the Army's treatment of the Indians, so he went his own way. That is the goal, isn't it? Everybody must learn to go his own way and follow his own truth. (How one does that can often be the question.) The Colonel turned his back on the war with the Indians, turned his back on the military and turned his back on the government. War—and its equivalent—was never to be mentioned in his house. That was *his* truth. What else did the Colonel do? He left. He left the people—the crowd—behind and he went over the mountains "to lose the madness." That is the deed all of us must do. We need to go to the place where we can follow our truth in order to lose the madness of the modern world.

What a statement. The Colonel, in this sense, is the individuating man. Notice the tense. Using the present tense, he's still at it. We know there is more to learn. A great deal will be said about that later.

It is wonderful the way "his going his own way" is said and felt in this film. The Colonel showed his uniqueness, and the tone is set. He is beyond the ordinary. He is not a man of the masses. He is bigger than life. For the Colonel, it was a midlife crisis, a change of direction, and a radical break with the past. For him it meant putting the military and the madness behind and—best of all—getting to the other side of the mountains. If you take "to get to the other side of the mountains" symbolically, it can mean many things, even if you are literally on a beach. And, Jung's use of "the other side" as referring to the unconscious is to give the other side a chance to speak, especially after a life of one-sided rationalism.

Notice the wording. The Colonel does not "kill the madness." He goes away to "lose the madness." If he went to "kill the madness" he would be acting just as the military. If you kill the thing you are trying to get away from, you become what you kill. You become what you are running from. That's why Jung said to be careful of what you fight against.

For example, Stalin was the great freedom fighter in Russia against the tyranny of the Czars, and then the "freedom fighter," Stalin, killed millions. The Colonel did not try to "kill the madness"—to do that would bring him closer to war and closer to the military, not separate from it. You have to watch how close you get to things. In a wonderful, soulful way, this distinction shows us the brutality and violence of war with so much more feeling. This is a movie that hates war. It is not a war movie. That is a big distinction.

In our modern war-facing world, Colonel Ludlow can be quite a model. How many of us really know the madness of the modern world and go against it? Or, do we just adapt? Or even feel helpless? We needn't be.

Let us return to the opening lines of the film again to consider what it says to us. The narrator is One Stab:

"Some people hear their own inner voices with great clearness and they live by what they hear. Such people become crazy or

they become legends. Tristan Ludlow was born in the moon of the falling leaves. It was a terrible winter. His mother almost died bringing him into this world. His father, the Colonel, brought him to me and I wrapped him in a bearskin and held him all that night. As he grew into a man, I taught him the great joy of the kill—when a hunter cuts out its warm heart, and holds it in his hands, setting its spirit free. Colonel Ludlow had three sons, but Tristan was his favorite. I had had sons too. But they are gone now, forever. It was a very bad time. The Colonel had tried to help the people, but it was no use. So he decided to go his own way. He wanted to lose the madness over the mountains, he said, and begin again. Lose the madness, he said.

And so we lived for many years, and the boys grew strong. Alfred was the older brother, old even for his years. Samuel was the youngest. There was nothing these brothers would not do for him. They watched over him like a treasure.

One year—I am an old man, and can not remember the year—but it was the moon of the red grass when Isabel Ludlow, their mother, went away for the winter. She said that the winters were too cruel for her. She said she was afraid of the bears. She was a strange woman anyway. That spring, though, she did not return, and after that she did not come much to see us. Alfred wrote her many letters, but Tristan refused to speak of her. His world was with me. Every warrior hopes a good death will find him but Tristan couldn't wait. He went looking for his."

[Tristan's encounter with the bear was as a young boy: He approaches a sleeping bear, and touches the bear. The bear awakens and pursues him, slashing his arm with his great paw. Tristan slashes back with his hunting knife, severing one of the bear's claws. The bear limps away.]

The Colonel: Tristan! Tristan! Was it a bear?
Tristan: Yes, sir.
Colonel: Can you breathe?
Tristan: Yes.
Colonel: Take your hand away, Take it away. [Sees the wound.] Ah, boy, you're a stupid half-breed jackass, did you know that?
Tristan: Yes, sir.

Colonel: One Stab put you up to this? He deserves to be dead, you know that.
[Turns to One Stab.] God knows how you've lived this long.
One Stab:[Speaks in his own language in reply.]
Colonel: You'll be all right, son.

[One Stab finds the claw, shows Tristan the bear claw, pats his back with pride, and laughs. The Colonel smiles.]

✤ ✤ ✤ ✤ ✤ ✤ ✤ ✤ ✤

One Stab: "I held these letters, many letters. Read them. They are from all of them—Ludlow, Isabel, Samuel, and the whole family. The whole story. It is all written here."

Do you get the feeling that this is more than just a primitive, brooding, hopeless love story? We haven't gotten to the romance yet, because Susannah hasn't yet arrived, but someone has already left—Isabel, the mother. If we take von Franz seriously, and believe that movies can be like fairy tales or dreams, we also remember that Jung talks about the number four as being the symbol of wholeness in the unconscious. In this story, notice that all four are masculine—the Colonel and his three sons. Not only that, there is a striking scene in which the feminine figure, the mother, departs. Isabel Ludlow, (who One Stab says was "strange anyway") would have to be very strange indeed to leave her children for the civilities of the East Coast, even though it was customary in those days, according to Harrison. What does that tell us about her warmth and her ability to nurture her young family? Something is missing, isn't it?

If you take the number symbolism to a deeper level, it points more specifically to the modern problem of the absent feminine, the problem with which this family is going to struggle. The dilemma begins when the woman does arrive on the scene and, predictably, she is not able to solve the problem or make up for this existing lack. The author's thesis is that the masculine foursome in the film points out the absent feminine. This film addresses something straight out of the unconscious—the modern problem that Jung has addressed at length. Movies are forms of our own myths, and establishing the right relationship to the feminine can be the number one problem in the modern world. This movie portrays that problem.

Now what does that mean? What do we mean by the right relationship to the feminine? What has been missing in the collective consciousness of our time?
  a.) Honoring Eros, relatedness, feeling discrimination and feeling values.
  b.) Paying attention to our guts, rather than to our heads.
  c.) Paying attention to our instincts rather than to what we think.
  d.) Paying attention to how our guts react rather than how we are supposed to react.
  e.) Getting down to our lower chakras, in the language of *kundalini* yoga, to feel the body again.

The Colonel and his three sons—Alfred, Samuel, and Tristan—are the four masculine characters confronting this problem of the feminine. This film reflects exactly what has been going on in the collective unconscious, which means in everybody, men and women. By paying attention to this story, you can get a deeper feeling for what is going on in you and in the collective.

First, you should notice what touches you. It is a matter of feeling—when your feeling is touched, and you feel it, and notice it. Remember that noticing is not automatic. In fact, half of our species walks around without noticing. You might see someone being touched by something in life, and you can ask him or her, "Hey, what's that?" But the reply you get is "I don't know." Then you ask, "Why are you crying?" The reply is still, "I don't know." By then you have to conclude, "Well, whom am I supposed to ask?" The fact is, we are not residents in our own house. We talk about exploring outer space, and going to the bottom of the sea, and climbing Mt. Everest, etc., but how about closer to home? We are what we will have all of our lives. Doesn't it make sense to know yourself and your reactions? The only way to do that is to notice your own reactions.

You will be amazed at what happens when you do that. You will have adventures in your life. For example, I know someone who has collected quite a bit of art over the years, and people who go by his house say, "Oh, you must know a lot about art." He does *not* know a lot about art. He just knows what he likes and he has good taste. That is all. He doesn't collect art because of knowledge. He knows what touches him, and what grabs his attention. Jung has a great mantra, which, if you follow it, it will lead you to great adventures for your entire life. He said, "Follow the feeling. Follow the feeling wherever it leads you." That's it. Follow the feeling. That is what the friend's art collection is all about—his feeling. He paid attention; he followed it and was glad that he did. (There is a great deal of difference between "the feeling" in the sense Jung meant it—of "feeling value within yourself,"—and of following the feeling of the moment. There is a big difference. Jung's was a deep truth; the other is a whim. But more about these distinctions later.)

So often we don't pay attention. We put things on the shelf, thinking "someday." The result is a collection of the same items on our shelves gathering dust. Instead, we should honor the feeling we have for this experience because that feeling carries gold for us. Actually, that experience happened to me with this film. I knew when I first saw the movie that I would need to do further work on it because it had gripped me so intensely. But, I put it on that shelf. It was only years later, at a random vote for further material, that the women in the audience voted for *"Legends."* The women led me to my own "neglected shelf." That is a great paradigm if enough men would listen.

Listen to what Edward Zwick—the director of this film—wrote about the musical score composed by James Horner:

> Somehow James managed to distill all those [our] lofty conversations into a score that is at once both brooding and lush, redolent of both love and loss, and that touches that secret place of awe I had experienced only once before—upon my first reading of *Legends of the Fall.*

Notice the phrase, "that touches the secret place of awe." It is particularly striking because Zwick talked about what this music did for him, what this story did for him. The definition of the religious instinct for Jung was what he called the *numinous*. The numinous is the place that inspires awe. Here, the director of this movie describes his feeling, and one gets the sense he was really touched by the numinous. He brings that same touch to us as we watch his film of the story, which had touched this feeling of awe in him.

Edward Edinger has written about the plays of the human psyche, the sacred games and ritual drama, and Edinger said that it is indicative of their psychological similarity that we refer to both games and drama with the same word, "play." "These action forms give human energy a second world in which to function. We are apt to forget the crucial role that games and athletic contests played in civilizing the aggressive energies of early man." In *"Homer's Contest,"* Friedrich Nietzsche described for us the Greek rituals of aggression in war:

> Why must Greek sculpture give form again and again to war and combat in innumerable repetitions? Distended human bodies—their sinews tense with hatred or the arrogance of triumph—writhing bodies, dying bodies, expiring. Why did the whole Greek world exalt over the combat scenes of the *Iliad*? I fear that we do not understand these in a sufficiently Greek manner. Indeed that we should shudder if we were to ever understand them in Greek.

Edinger reflects: "It is these wild and primitive energies that are contained, channeled and finally transformed by means of organized games and athletic contests. The Greeks did it very well. In the beginning, the games were always dedicated to a god, indicating that the athletes' efforts were being offered up to a transpersonal meaning. Indeed, a transpersonal meaning is achieved whenever we succeed in transforming primitive psychic energy by humanizing it."

Let me repeat those last words: *"Transpersonal meaning is achieved whenever we succeed in transforming primitive psychic energy by humanizing it."* This sentence touches on two of the big problems facing our modern civilization. It is also what our movie is about.

First, most people are not in touch with their primitive energies. We don't know our bear, or tiger, or wolf in order to be able to contain or transform them. On the other hand, and at the opposite extreme, is the drug culture or the subculture, which is about getting in touch with that primitive energy to experience it, because the old way has stifled it. It can be a legitimate attempt to touch back into those primitive psychic energies, but the problem becomes what to do with them once you find them. The drug subculture has no answer for that. These energies need to be contained. They need to be channeled and humanized. That transformation is what "makes" a person, and also what makes him bigger.

Colonel Ludlow espouses that in this film. It is the father, the Colonel, who had met the wild and primitive energies of war, of grizzlies, of Indians, and he was not broken by them. He threw down his sword, and said, "No more." He walked away. He went his own way. Because he left, he captured and distilled within his own personality the Self, with a capital S. He distilled within his own personality the center that contains that transpersonal meaning. In this story, Colonel Ludlow is a representative of the Self. He speaks with a wisdom that his sons often hate. They get angry with his truth. They think he is an old gruff. They think he is out of the flow of things. Yet in every case, he is absolutely prophetic, and it comes back to haunt his children. He was generally on target about everything, except of course, about Tristan.

Tristan is the one who—as One Stab says—is the rock upon which many were broken. The most obvious interpretation is that love can be a rock that breaks us. The alchemists also spoke about being broken—they believed getting broken was a necessary process because it opened you up. It wasn't charming and it didn't feel good, but it opened you up to transformation. In fact, the alchemists insisted that being broken was the only way transformation could happen. The dominant myth of Western civilization is the story of Jesus, which tells us that He was the original broken one. Jesus was the one broken for us, echoing the words of the Psalms and the prophet Isaiah from the Old Testament. One Stab's words reverberate the psychic reality of brokenness. There is much wisdom in his words. One Stab, too, carries the Self in this sense. (For further study on the alchemists, refer to Edinger's *Anatomy of the Psyche.*)

So what can we say about Tristan? Big personalities are often the rocks that break others. Tristan was a big personality—the personality of this story. Jesus was like that. He was a star. He was the rock, the stone, the original one. Jung was also like that—people couldn't take him. He was dismissed. He still is. If you are attracted to a rock, or if you are lying in the riverbed, you need to be careful because that is where you can get broken, One Stab tells us. Pay attention to the rocks and do not let them break you unless you know it is your fate. In that case, you can't do anything about it; you will be broken anyway because it is your fate.

This film is rich and full of the essence of myth. I think we can learn much from it. As Edinger concludes:
"Myths are not simply tales of happenings in the remote past, but eternal dramas that are living themselves out repeatedly in our own personal lives and in what we see all around us. To be aware of this adds a dimension to existence that is usually reserved for the poets. To the extent that we can cultivate awareness of this transpersonal dimension, life is enlarged and broadened. Just as Moses is eternally bringing down the law from Sinai, and Jesus is forever being crucified and resurrected, so Heracles is eternally performing his labors, Perseus is still confronting Medusa, and Theseus is forever stalking the Minotaur. All these dramas are happening in and around us constantly. They are eternal patterns of the way life happens below the surface, if only one can see it." (*The Eternal Drama*, page 3.)

The Colonel is still going to face his journey to go to the other side of the mountains. Tristan will still have to wrestle with the bear, and Alfred will still have to deal with his deadly jealousy over Susannah. And Susannah will have to carry her own betrayal.

It is from this perspective—myth as mirror of the psyche and as eternal dramas being repeated—that we approach this wonderful movie, because the film mirrors much about the psyche in the modern world.

2

Fathers and Sons

Track 3,
Off To War

It seemed synchronistic that Saturn and Jupiter, the two big astrological planets of fatherhood, were active in the skies as we were preparing this material. Saturn is usually seen as the more negative, constricting planet that insists on rules and responsibilities. Like anything else, if Saturn is related to, he is not negative at all, but a helper who aids us with carrying out our responsibilities. But when we shirk our duties—if we have a tendency to shirk them—Saturn will persecute us all our lives. Then he becomes the great negative one.

Jupiter, on the other hand, is usually seen as more benevolent. The Colonel would certainly fit in Jupiter's category. Jupiter is more like the benevolent father, the giver of largesse and good fortune. He is very helpful. However, like Saturn, Jupiter can also turn horribly negative if one does not relate to him, and he converts us into being wasteful or impulsive or manic as well.

Nevertheless, Jupiter and Saturn are two powerful father images which the skies have given us as we begin this journey. Keep them in mind during our trip through *Legends of the Fall* because they can provide very helpful insights into the challenge of fatherhood. You, the reader, might want to know where they are astrologically when you read this material.

This movie is a noteworthy example of the relationship that exists between a father and his sons. In honor of that—and in honor of the wonderful short story by Ernest Hemingway—we've entitled this chapter "Fathers and Sons." The action of the film develops around the three sons coming up against the father, and what happens to each of them in the process. This unfolding is central to the entire story. This, too, shows the Fall. All does not go well.

The power of this movie is that it gets you in touch with the feeling side of life. For many of us that is a foreign land. Instead of an intellectual exercise, this film can provide an active way for us to figuratively cut our heads off—which is where most of us hang out—and to drop down into the regions of our body below the neck. That can be a very difficult thing to do and it often requires a concerted conscious effort. One visual way of imagining that is to drop down into your stomach, to literally practice that. Once you are able to do that, you will find that you have yet another task awaiting you, the task of discrimination.

The problem of discrimination means separating out one thing from another—in this case, feelings from emotions. This movie introduces us to that task in a big way. Its central theme is about Eros, feeling, feelings, and emotions; each is different from the other. Consider that for a moment. Eros is about being "connected" to another; feeling is how we value that connection. Feeling is different from "feelings" and feelings are different from emotions. Sorting out all of this is very important to our conscious awareness of who we are, because consciousness is about discrimination. It is about seeing what this is and what that is. We will try to make this clear without getting too complicated, and we will see how all of these distinctions resolve in the family of Colonel Ludlow and his three sons.

Eros is the god of relatedness who makes connections. It has been suggested to you already that it is important to notice in a theater or a movie what specifically attracts you. Jung tells us that we are attracted psychologically to what we need, or lack, and that we are repelled by the opposite—that which we already have or do not like in ourselves. Eros is that active power operating behind the scenes to throw us into life. Eros doesn't care if life is messy. In fact, sometimes one suspects that Eros likes it messy—the messier the better. Some of us have been sitting on our shelves like laboratory bottles, and it takes a lot of mess to get us moving again. So Eros, the god—and the god of this film, *Legends of the Fall*—throws people into life. How does Eros operate? The *anima* in men, and the *animus* in women—those contrasexual elements in each of us that Jung talks about (cf glossary)—will do everything they can to involve us in our relationships and in life. Suddenly we are captivated or irresistibly drawn—by what we love or by what we hate. For example, in the film, Susannah has Samuel "spinning." At the same time, he is caught up in the war in Europe. The result is a mess. Actually, Susannah is so beautiful, so charming, and so feminine that she has the whole family "spinning"—not just Samuel. Susannah, here, carries Eros for all of the men—and they, individually, will have to sort it out.

This takes discrimination, as we see early in the movie with Samuel. He might be the metaphor for a lot of us in our naïveté. Samuel is full of naïveté and idealism. He is blinded by his idealism. Jung has said that the more you constellate the light—that is to say, the more you identify with being on the "right side" or the "just side," or morally good and upright, as Samuel does—the more you must be careful, because the darkness is always right behind. (That does not mean we are to be lazy or half-witted, but it does say to us that we need to be alert and responsible to what we're about, and not be naïve.)

Naïveté can be the particular vice of Christianity. Christians often get lulled into the belief that if they pray and do their work, that "someone"—perhaps an angel—will take care of them. For many, this is a tenet of their faith. This naïveté was the same for Mary Baker Eddy and the Christian Scientists. Those who have lived long enough know that the angels bail out at significant times. It is naïve to be lulled into idealism or into an optimism that always expects the best out of life. Jung warns us against it. Jung says that going hand-in-hand with Tristan the lover is Tristan, the berserk. Craziness is not far behind, to use the metaphor of the movie. Unlike Tristan, Samuel must learn to discriminate and learn to use the feeling function. Tragically, he doesn't. Because hand in hand with Samuel the poet and idealist, is Samuel on the front lines of a war he doesn't understand.

When we say "feeling," or to "follow the feeling," we don't mean feelings or emotions. We are not talking of feelings merely in a vague, sentimental and popular sense. It is not enough to speak of rash feelings or guilty feelings or hurt feelings. It is not enough to encourage someone to express their feelings. Some sort of theoretical understanding is also required for the word "feeling." Here we rely on Jung's theory of types, and specifically, the feeling function or function of valuing. What we do mean is that deep valuing center within you that knows what you want and what you need. The feeling function of discrimination is that function of value, which says, "This is important to me," or conversely, "This is not important to me." It is the function of value, of placing value on things. To know what one values is a necessity for consciousness and for individuation. Samuel is naïve and carried away by his idealism. He does not know what he is doing and he does not know what he values. Had he known, he might have asked, "What does this say about my relationship with Susannah?" Then he really would have been in the "soup." Instead, he didn't ask the question and tragically avoided the issues it would have raised. Many of us do that all the time, especially when we refuse to question our idealism, to question our feeling.

One of the central scenes of this film is the mother's leaving, which causes the absence of the feminine. The feminine, according to Jung, is the principal carrier of Eros. You don't need to know psychology or to understand intellectually that the principal characters in this story are going to encounter some huge obstacles and get broken because of her absence. The film lets you know that in spades. There is no mediating feminine in this film, no one to mediate the opposites. Everyone is torn apart. When the feminine does show up, it does so in the person of Susannah, who we learn right off is "frail." And we see what happens to her. (Pet and little Isabel are other issues.)

The bear is the great animal of this film. It is also a huge symbol. A bear, especially a grizzly bear, is a huge animal. Anyone who has been close to one in the wild (like in Yellowstone or Glacier National Park or Alaska) knows the immensity of it. Camping out in Yellowstone years ago, we came to know the immense power of the wild with that animal around. The big grizzly bear is here for all to see in the opening scene of this movie. Perhaps it can convey to you the sense of terror of this huge, immense, overpowering energy. A bear has enormous emotion and power and the scene depicts that rather well. The psychological sin, and the Freudian error, is to reduce the bear symbolically when we say, "Well, he could stand for this or he could stand for that." That is not the way to approach the bear. You need here to see the bear in his whole entity coming at you *to feel* that enormity in this scene.

One of the words we use about this animal is "berserk," a German-rooted word that was looked upon as a positive quality by the Germans in olden times. (ber=bear; serk=skin or shirt= bear shirts or berserk.)We use the word berserk when we "lose it," when we lose control of our emotions and our feelings. It can actually be a very invigorating experience to lose it like that, to really lose it all the way—to go berserk in our anger, consciously and deliberately. That is an encounter with the bear, consciously having a huge emotional reaction. That confrontation is akin to what Nietzsche described when he described the Greeks at war, letting their aggression and hatred flow fully.

As we see here in this scene, Tristan was initiated into that encounter at an early age, as a young "warrior," with One Stab's encouragement.

Imagination can help here. Put yourself in the scene. Close your eyes and imagine that scene of the boy Tristan and the bear. Pretend you are Tristan's mother or Tristan's father and you see Tristan going after that bear. What is your first response without thinking? Not what you think in your head but your gut reaction? How many of us would pass the One Stab test of being thrilled with Tristan? Few, because most of us are afraid of such physical danger. We might react just as the parent, Colonel Ludlow, did. That is a real test of our instincts. Not many of us are so in touch with the natural order of things as is an American Indian like "One Stab."

It was the test of a young boy's character, an initiation into real manhood and physical danger, and not withdrawing from it. That is why One Stab was so proud of Tristan, and so thrilled that Tristan came away from the encounter with the claw of that bear. One Stab was filled with pride, and patted him on the back. Then, if you remember, the camera pans over to the face of the father, the Colonel—who had just called Tristan a stupid jackass and said that he deserved to be dead. Then for an instant, you saw a hidden smile on the Colonel's face, and you saw his pride in his son. That is a moment which contains the opposites. The Colonel reacted exactly as a parent must, yet also knew One Stab's truth as well. Amazing and wonderful.

That is a key moment which passes between fathers and sons in which the father has to call his son a stupid jackass, yet is still proud of him at the same time. It is that subtle boundary where a father does not kill the son's spirit, but lets him know the line of danger. It is a powerful scene, worth a great deal of reflection and worth the attention of fathers. We are good at the "jackass" part, but not the pride.

Let us now go back to the film to some other scenes in which the plot regarding relationships develops. It begins with the arrival of Susannah. The Colonel has just written to Isabel, his wife. He has expressed his misgivings over having raised their sons alone in Montana. Isabel—now living in the East—replies:

> Dear William, you take too much responsibility upon yourself as always. Our sons are finding their own paths. They are willful, certainly, but then who are you and I to complain of willfulness? As for Samuel, I have big news. At a Harvard tea for Amy Lowell, he met and instantly loved Miss Susannah Fincannon. And William, I know it will surprise you greatly, but they are engaged. He will bring her to Montana this summer to introduce her to his brothers, and to you. So William, please behave yourself, and be as charming as only you can be.

[The train arrives, bringing Samuel and Susannah to Montana.]
Alfred: Hey! There he is. How the hell are you?
Samuel: I'm good, and you?
Colonel: Samuel.
Samuel: How are you, father?
Colonel: Good to see you, boy.
Samuel: Good to see you.
[Susannah has disembarked, shyly greets Alfred] Hello.
Samuel: [Suddenly remembering Susannah, and that she has not met his family] Oh, Father. This is my fiancée, Susannah.
Susannah: Hello.
Colonel: Miss Fincannon.
Susannah: I am pleased to meet you. [Warmly said, she then kisses the Colonel's cheek]
Colonel: [Taken by surprise, he blusters] It's an honor.
Samuel: And this is Alfred.
Susannah: Hello.

Alfred: How do you do?
Porter: Here's your dog, Miss.
Susannah: Thank you. [Comment in background: "Dog? It looks like a horse!"]
Alfred: That's a strange looking animal.
Susannah: This is Finn. He's a champion, aren't you Finn?
Alfred: You really like exotic looking dogs then, Miss Fincannon?
Susannah: Very much, Mr. Ludlow. Please, call me Susannah.
Alfred: All right.
Samuel: He's just plain old Alfred.
Alfred: You shut up.
Colonel: Where's Tristan?
Alfred: Ah, he's off somewhere. You know him.
Colonel: Well he'll be here tonight to welcome his brother home or I'll know the reason why. Well, Miss Fincannon. Please. [He offers her his arm, and escorts her to the waiting car] Did you have a good journey?

Isabel's letter to the Colonel continues:

She is such a lovely creature, William. But I fear the loss of her parents has given her a certain fragility, and at times, I think she feels very alone in the world. But she has found a new family now, hasn't she?

[The family is riding from the station to the homestead. The boys are on horseback. Susannah and the Colonel ride in the open car driven by One Stab. Samuel begins talking to Alfred about the events in Europe]

Samuel: The German military are ready to use chaos in Croatia as a justification for actions that will plunge the civilized world into absolute—"
Colonel: Samuel! The word civilized has no place in any discussion of the affairs of this world.
Alfred: [To Samuel] Just forget it. [Changes subject] Miss Fincannon, Mother has told us of your sympathies with the Social Reformers.

Susannah: [Laughs] You make it sound like a disease.
Alfred: Oh, no. No, on the contrary, I'm in agreement.
Susannah: Well, your mother has told me about One Stab. She said that he was a great warrior.
Alfred: Ah, yes. He has a bag of scalps hidden away somewhere to prove it, too. But don't worry. He's devoted to father now, or rather they are devoted to each other.
Susannah: Can he speak English?
Alfred: Stab? Speak English? He wouldn't lower himself to speak English, would you, Stab? [Stab replies in his native language.] But watch out, because he understands it perfectly well.
Samuel: Hey! There's Tristan! [Gallops off to meet Tristan, who approaches on horseback, bringing up a trail pony behind him]
Tristan: Don't they feed you up there? [Dismounts, embraces Samuel.]
Samuel: Not much. Ah, you smell.
Tristan: Missed me, did you? [They approach the car.] And you have a girl.
Samuel: Isn't she amazing?
Susannah: So this is Tristan...and does he speak English? [Tristan stands silently looking at her]
Alfred: Tristan, for God's sake! [Pours water over the sweaty and smelly Tristan] [All laugh. Tristan collects himself]
Tristan: Miss Fincannon. It is a pleasure to meet you. I hope that you and Ugly here find every happiness together. [He then speaks in native language to One Stab, in obvious appreciation of Miss Fincannon.]
Alfred: Don't mind my brother. Your dog has more breeding than he has.

[Tristan grabs Alfred down from his horse and wrestles him to the ground. All the brothers engage in horseplay.]

There is the introduction to the family. Susannah arrives, and everything is set in motion.

There are a couple of things not very obvious in the film, which are written in the book. The first is that Isabel, the mother, has virtually set Samuel up. Mothers have a hard time staying out of the picture, even when they are on the East Coast. The author, Jim

Harrison, calls Isabel an early feminist, and presumably—now living on the East Coast, around all that culture—sending Samuel to Harvard was part of her agenda. So when she writes the Colonel about the sons being willful, she knows firsthand of what she speaks (not that the Colonel doesn't.) There, the mother is acting behind the scenes.

But it is nice to see the brothers and their camaraderie. There is much interplay between them and with their father, who is very formal, and obviously not too comfortable with the feminine of the species, Susannah. The Colonel is very formal and stiff and uncertain in that encounter with her. His is not the realm of feeling and warmth. He has written to Isabel of his uncertainty, of raising the boys in this wild and untamed place without her. Yet as the father, he is the initiator, the challenger, the foil against which the sons struggle. He is the giver of spirit and vision. He is not the giver of connection and warmth. Anthony Hopkins, Colonel Ludlow—from England, from Cornwall (which synchronistically is also the setting of the myth of *Tristan and Isolde*)—carries that formality and discomfort in his bearing throughout this scene.

Samuel, the youngest, is filled with Eastern thoughts and he soon becomes consumed with the idea of the impending war. At dinner that night there is the beginning of the confrontation between the father and son, which soon erupts into open conflict as Samuel breaks the news of his support of the war. His father explodes, "There will be no talk of war in this family!" Samuel is insulted, outraged by his father's intractability, shouting back, "It's the war to end all wars!" and "we have to be involved," "we have to be up-to-date." That is the cry of the young—"we have to be up to date." Alfred takes his brother's side there. The Colonel remains unmoved, standing his ground. He will hear no more of the war. Samuel, defiant, throws down the gauntlet and declares, "I am going to Canada to enlist!"

We need to step back and notice the timing of this declaration. It is quite shocking in the context of the story. Samuel has just arrived with Susannah, his intended, this "amazing" woman, who has him "spinning." Now suddenly, his idealism about the war inflames him and he is going to Canada to enlist. We notice by her reaction that Susannah has heard nothing of this. Immediately upon making his announcement, Samuel realizes his difficulty that he had forgotten to mention any of his plans to Susannah. He proceeds and commits a great sin against Eros. He has brought this woman clear across the country and yet has chosen not to involve her in this huge plan of his heart. Indeed, he had decided it without her. It is a riveting moment. Susannah is obviously devastated. In that moment, there is a vacuum, and the god Eros is not present. In that moment, several things begin to happen.

Samuel is filled with an idea. He is full of enthusiasm and he "is filled with a god"—what the Greeks called *en theos*. But it can be a dark god, darkened by passion. When that passion happens, the idea is not contained. It breaks the container and carries the person away. Samuel is naïve and idealistic, and is carried away by his fiery obsession with the menace of foreign adversaries and a colossal war to end all wars. The Colonel, just like a real father, erupts with all the opposition he can muster: "No!" But Samuel, just like a young son, says, "Yes!" anyway.

It is again to the Colonel's credit—and it takes a great deal of masculine strength to do this at this moment—that he does not crush Samuel. He does not overwhelm his son. He does not stop him. He simply leaves the room even though it is very clear how he feels. And everyone knows—just as the Colonel knows—that Samuel is going to suffer the consequences. We know that Samuel is going to "get it." Once again, there is a very interesting sequence in the book that is not in the movie. In the book, Colonel Ludlow has a dream that night, a nightmare that wakes him up. He sees his son killed by the war. Whether symbolically, or metaphorically, the war destroys Samuel. Colonel Ludlow has to struggle with that dream.

Here is the man who has stood against war and turned his back on it. Isn't it heartbreaking that this would be the very issue which now arises in the family? That's the way it works, however. You can be sure that the very issue you think you have resolved will come back into the family to be worked out. The shadow of the family will erupt. The shadow of the family will be carried by one of the children, the one who carries the shadow of the parents. In this case, it is Samuel, because as the book makes very clear, it is Samuel who is aligned with his mother. He is not the father's son. The father's son is Tristan.

And what of Alfred? Poor Alfred is left to flounder. He is left out of the picture. In fact, One Stab says of Alfred in the beginning, "He was old even in his youth." In some people, to be old even in their youth can be a healthy thing, but that is not what One Stab means here. Alfred's oldness is not healthy. In fact, the contentiousness in Alfred—his struggle throughout the entire story—is to find his place, his birthright. And so, here he sides with Samuel. He does not yet know where his place is. He doesn't get it until the last scene.

Throughout the story Alfred is presented as the sober one, the methodical one, the rule carrier. He is the responsible one, involved in business. He is also running for public office and working in government, all to his father's dismay—and he is rather boring. He is *always* nearby. The book calls him stodgy and methodical. He is duty-bound, caught in the old and caught by the old. However, as the first-born son, he does not carry the usual task of the eldest in families and in institutions until the very end of the story.

The father carries the old. The Colonel has carried his conflict with war and government and has worked it out for himself, but he cannot give his clarity to his sons. It is not alive for them just because the father experienced it. And it is much less alive for Samuel, who has been away at school on the East Coast near his mother.

A parent cannot pass his experience on to his children—they have to get their own experience, even if it means reinventing the wheel. The parents cannot pass the wheel on, even though they would like to give them this cloak and say "Now: you can be an adult. We've gone through all of this already, and now you have graduated." It doesn't work that way. It doesn't happen, even though parents have the irresistible urge to try and do it anyway. The father, Colonel Ludlow, has worked through this whole issue of war, and has established his homestead as a monument against the war and government and bureaucracy and institutional living. Now the youngest son throws it in his face, and says "I'm going to enlist," and Alfred joins in, "I'm going with him." To his eternal credit, Colonel Ludlow takes it like a good and noble father. He arranges for the horses, and sends his sons off to war, bidding them safe return even though his heart is breaking, because he knows. Not only that, he asks Tristan to go to look after Samuel. It is interesting that he does not ask Alfred, even though Alfred has volunteered to go with Samuel. The Colonel asks Tristan instead to look after and to take care of Samuel. It is that pledge which eventually breaks Tristan's spirit. The Colonel does not ask Alfred, because intuitively he knows where Alfred stands. And, unlike Tristan, it is not with the father.

Tristan's imagined inability to live up to that impossible promise to his father wounds him and breaks his spirit. That is when the bear threatens to overwhelm him. Who of us have not made impossible promises, which we cannot keep? Remember the line at the beginning of the film, "Some people hear their own inner voices with great clearness and they live by what they hear. Such people become crazy or they become legends." That is Tristan's task: to learn from his inner voices. It is the task of individuation and the work of analysis. The whole process is about listening to your own inner voices with clarity, learning to discriminate and not being overwhelmed by craziness.

When one does that, Edward Edinger says, "Transpersonal meaning is achieved." Do you remember that sentence? "Transpersonal meaning is achieved whenever we succeed in transforming primitive psychic energy by humanizing it." Edinger means that transformation keeps your crazy side, the overwhelming power of the unconscious, your bear, from devouring you. You must work with it. When you get hold of and use your psychic energy, put it into your creativity and into your life. This energy has power. It works and has effects. That is what made Tristan so unique, wasn't it? He was the wild one but he was distinctive. Ask the women, if you don't believe that statement.

We won't even mention Tristan's (Brad's) looks because we are supposed to be getting past appearances, and emphasis on aesthetics. Well, yes and no. Don't forget about appearances altogether. Very often appearances are our first clue of what attracts us. Don't turn into an elite or spiritual snob and say, "I'm not interested in that" or "it gets in the way." Oh, yes, we are interested. And if we are not, then our animus or anima will be. We cannot avoid it and if the anima or animus gets it with the "appearance contest," then we will become overwhelmed and the consequences won't be pretty. Appearances let us know what does and does not attract us. Remember—Eros is about throwing us into life, and Eros is not concerned if our life becomes messy. We might be concerned, but Eros is not.

Transpersonal meaning is achieved when we sit down and work with these enormous energies. If you teach, use your energy to teach.

Hold your primitive psychic energy and use it in your teaching. For example, in a recent interview, the actor Mel Gibson said that acting was his way of keeping what he called his "Viking Crazy Man" in control—that he could "stare it down when it's reaching out its hand to grab me." He puts that energy into his acting. Then his acting has power. What a wonderful example. His case is not about "doing art." It is about doing whatever you are creatively doing in your life and using the energy of these forces by containing them. A great example of containing the energies is a paranoid schizophrenic trumpet player who becomes transformed when playing; he is sick when not playing. That is Tristan's task and life work—to learn to use his bear energy. It is the same task for all of us—to learn to use the archetypal energy we have.

We could use Tristan as a symbol for that task that many of us face, though a small number of us do not. The task, the problem, the difficulty, the challenge par excellence is: how does one approach the live wire of nuclear, psychic energy, and not get consumed and/or burnt up by this enormous energy? That is the question for enormously talented people who have enormous energy—people like Tristan, Jim Harrison, Leonard Bernstein or Beethoven. These artists have an enormous connection to the creative source of the collective unconscious. How do/did they use that energy without being burned up by it? (Although none escape without some "burns.")

We all know hundreds of examples of creative people. Hollywood stars are daily gossip column fodder for this. So too, are athletic professionals, paid millions of dollars fresh out of college, who have been "burned" in their personal lives. Or to put it another way, they are stars on one level and disasters on another. The trick is to be good on both levels, professional and personal. One common cop-out is to say in effect, "I'm a star, so deal with my bad behavior." Naturally those who have to do so, resent it, as they should.

On the other hand it is possible that the enormous energy and adaptation it takes to be a "star" leaves little left over for the adaptation to ordinary life. Choices will then have to be made. For example, it would be much better for a man's wife—say the poet, artist, William Blake's—if he could say to her, "I know I'm miserable as a husband. Thank you for being able to put up with me." Sadly, though, that does not often happen because people are not aware of themselves. For the sake of real relationships, the other party needs to know the enormous price paid for the enormous talent, which can lead to the enormous suffering the spouse will encounter. (For further reflection, refer to Jung's *Essay on Literature and Art,* CW 14.)

"Nothing is free in life. And the more valuable it is, the more expensive it is." (Jung, Houston film interview.) People need to know such things and the price they will have to pay for the cost of fame, riches, or success.

The attractiveness of Tristan's personality is complicated by the fact of Brad Pitt's good looks. Women may have difficulty understanding why they are so attracted to him. The illusion is: good looks = glamour = power. But Tristan's initiation by the bear also meant "a hard fate"—a fate that at times was as overwhelming as a grizzly's energy. Some people get so hooked by power that they do not even see the hard fate that is involved. Take, for example, the leaders of big corporations and even countries. One has to be prepared and big enough to carry that much energy. People who want to be millionaires (usually because their ego is too small to begin with hoping that the projections of money will add to their size) sometimes crash miserably under the weight of that much wealth. It takes a large ego to handle large projects and large sums. Wealthy people are notorious for not being wealthy in how they relate to others. They are called "misers" or "Scrooges." Jesus knew of what He spoke when He said, "It is easier for a camel to get through the eye of a needle, than for a rich person to be happy" (quote modernized by author.) Who has ever said, "Beware of riches?"

What do we Tristan-wannabes need to do? We need to learn how to relate (connect, discuss, be aware of) our psychic energy. To use Edinger's words, we need to learn to humanize our psychic energies and to give them human form through our human personality. We need to use our energies that way, instead of being used by them. We need to fight with our "bear," not just give in. We need to learn to accept our "bear energy" and make friends with it instead of letting it explode in our families. We need to know what our instinctive energy is like. Jung says animals are good images of our instincts. So, draw your animal. Paint it, walk around it, and get to know it. That is a definite way to begin to humanize your inner animal and your inner energies.

Samuel, Alfred, and Tristan—the three sons—go to fight the war.

The Colonel, like a real father, has erupted internally, but stood his ground. They go to war over his objections. Not only has Samuel defied his father; he has also betrayed him, as well as Susannah, his beautiful fiancée, with whom everyone in the family is obviously smitten.

Samuel betrayed Susannah by turning his back on her, by making a secret deal with his inner anima and by deciding to go to war without telling her. He made a secret deal with the inner woman inside himself (his anima), not with his outer woman, Susannah. That habit is how men exclude the women in their lives all the time. That is also the reason woman so often go berserk while their men are scratching their heads. The men do not know what they do.

There is that word "berserk" again. It is a primitive reaction which comes from instinct. Women can smell the plot a mile away when a man is orchestrating a secret deal inside himself. Whether it is planning behind her back to watch the Super Bowl, or setting up a business deal, she knows when she is being excluded while the secret deal is being planned. Samuel decided to turn his back on Susannah and his father to go to war, to prove his mettle and his Eros against an unknown foe in an unknown land.

That brings up an interesting question. Why does he do it? Why now? We get a pretty clear hint in this film in his earlier conversation with Tristan outside on the lawn. As Alfred and Susannah play tennis, Samuel confides his sexual fears to Tristan. He tells Tristan how full of ideas and passion Susannah is, and he admits his misgivings, that he isn't sure if he can measure up. Keeping in mind the words of Nietzsche about the primitive masculine drive as depicted by the Greeks, and knowing that male aggression is one of the most problematical drives there is, one wonders if Samuel's decision to roar off to fight the war is not an unconscious attempt to allay his fears by proving his manhood in another arena, as well as a sly hint by Harrison, the author, about the role of the unconscious in fighting wars.

Masculine aggression is a major issue for men. What does man do with that fury? There are no wild bears to hunt anymore. Wars are not fought on battlefields as of old—rarely is there the type of warfare which once allowed the aggression to "flow fully." For example, being a couch potato and watching other guys get paid to do battle on a football field is not very engaging, especially here, for the body. So where does masculine aggression go?

Throughout this wretched episode of the movie, when one feels one already knows what is going to happen and how awful it is going to be, one cannot help but wish for the mediating influence of the feminine and/or of the mother who is not present. One wonders what could have happened if a real woman had been there, with a different perspective on going to war. We wonder if she would not have stepped in between these opposing men and come up with a surprising third opinion. That is the real place where the feminine can mediate a new view, something which is unexpected to everyone. It didn't happen here because the feminine in a real woman was not present. So nothing was mediated. It is worthwhile to reflect on that problem, even though it is pretty clear the die had been cast for Samuel.

✤ ✤ ✤ ✤ ✤ ✤ ✤ ✤ ✤

Here is a modern dream of a man, a father, which highlights the problem between fathers and sons:

> Grey-haired men in grey suits, grey ties, and shiny black shoes had taken over the backyard of my childhood home. They looked slick and professional, but they were demons of destruction. They had turned the garage into a chamber of torture and execution. Their task was to torture and then murder their rebellious, wild, creative young men. It seems they had been involved in this work for some time. When I arrive on the scene and realize what is going on, I am shocked but unable to do much about it. Their evil seems much too well established and beyond my control. Upon entering the garage, I am appalled to see Toby, a young man from my student days, who is about to be strapped to a conveyor belt and murdered. At the end of the belt is a huge mechanical saw which will cut him in two. I try to stop this from happening, but Toby is resigned to his fate and he even seems to be joking with his executioners. He is having a cigarette with them before the horror starts. He assumes that I cannot help and places himself on the belt ready to be killed. As I protest in rage, he is conveyed toward the saw, which I cannot see, because it is hidden in darkness.

That is the end of the dream. It is a terrible dream of the father problem—the grey-haired men in the dream—the destroyer of what is young and wild, and especially, what is creative. The trick is how to save both—the old and the young—and how to carry both. It is not easy for a lot of men. Our dreamer feels helpless in the face of this terrible issue confronting him. He must do something. Oversentimentalizing either the masculine or the feminine does not help. From therapeutic experience, I have learned that it is important for a lot of men to get in touch with their real masculinity and their rage, in this case, first. Toward the end of analysis comes the redemption of their inner feminine.

The feminine can be a rescuing symbol. As Marie-Louise von Franz describes in her wonderful book, *Individuation in Fairy Tales,* the feminine element is somewhat closer to the human, the ordinary, the dark and the imperfect. For example, in Roman Catholicism, Mary has traditionally played the role of mediator. When God the Father gets carried away, the petitioner prays to Mary to intercede, to calm him down and soften His judgment or His anger. The same thing happens in families, when the father is the disciplinarian—the mother has to step in, and calm things down. That can be so valuable.

The masculine, the Logos—the discriminating logic—often discriminates starkly, in terms of black and white. It sees things in the light of the Sun and it sees things very clearly. But that is not the only value. There is also another value of understanding the exceptions to white and black. That value is the feminine.

According to von Franz, women think in terms of exceptions. They do not think in terms of rules. If you don't believe that, just watch women drive. It is true and really funny. One can see the men all lined up in a row, keeping to their lanes, in line with the row of cars in front of them. Along comes a lady in her car and she just goes right through the traffic without a second look. This is not stated with sarcasm or with disdain. Instead, it is refreshing. It leaves the men exasperated, screaming and cursing. She is not following the rules. She simply cuts right through without a second thought.

Von Franz goes on to say that when one sees women who side with the masculine principle and condemn their children because they have broken a rule, you feel that something is amiss. It is a travesty of the feminine. If you are a woman, and you find that you are run by the rules, it means that the animus has taken over and you are not in your own centered place. According to von Franz, a woman herself, one can be sure when a woman makes a rule or believes in rules, that it is the animus in her who does so and not she herself. The more natural tendency of a woman is to think in exceptions and about what they feel is right, never mind who says what about it. (*Individuation in Fairy Tales*, pp. 19-21)

For psychological proof of the feminine principle, just look around. Von Franz has described it with regard to her own work. Quoting the alchemists in comparing her writings to Jung's writings, she said that Jung was the master. He was the teacher, the scholar, the brilliant one, the father—the one up there, and very abstract. She was the sister, the woman elucidator. She said that the woman's task was to bring things down to earth. That was what she tried to do in her writings, to bring Jung down to earth. She quoted an alchemical saying, "Man is the heaven of woman, and woman is the earth of man." (*Psychological Perspectives*, 1988)

"Man is the heaven of woman." A man who functions as a man can be the one who can give a woman spirit and a bigger vision. "Woman is the earth of man." A woman who functions as a woman can bring him down to earth and root him in the ordinary and the practical. Consequently, each task is very important. Unfortunately, the feminine element is missing in the Colonel's household, despite the presence of the Indian woman and her daughter, little Isabel. They do not have the function of mother and wife in the family. The inner feeling value within the home is missing. The feeling function is disturbed.

One has to be able to look within to find that value. According to von Franz, the mother is the one responsible for the invisible feeling tone within the home. She is the one who can create a certain atmosphere. She does so whether she sets about the task of doing it or not. The feeling atmosphere is vital. Today's emphasis on potty training and on feeding manuals—whether in Dr. Spock or John Rosemond—overlooks the importance of this in childcare. The emphasis today is on the practical and functional, not on the feeling atmosphere. Yet that is where the mother's role is so important. The inner feeling value and fantasy life of the mother is vital and necessary to life, not just the outer rule. If a mother is upset and struggling with darkness and depression, the child will also.

On the other hand, if her feeling tone is right, she can nourish the right adaptation in herself. She can trust her husband and her children, and her expectations of them will have a profound effect. Von Franz tells us that the mother must spin the right kind of fantasy, neither overvaluing nor undervaluing her child, keeping it rightly in her mind and heart. (*The Feminine in Fairy Tales*) Then the child can go his own way. In the story of Jesus, we read of how Mary "kept these things in her own heart" about her son, and when it was time for Him to face His ordeals, He was able to do that. That support is the feminine feeling value, which was missing in the Colonel's household.

It is also important for the father to tend to his unconscious fantasies, particularly toward his daughters. It is important to not let his anima fantasies get projected onto them. In this story, there are no daughters, and the Colonel's masculinity serves as the doorway through which his sons come to their own masculinity.

Samuel, the mother's son, has come back from the East filled with idealism, and bringing his fiancée, Susannah. His idealism leads him to abandon her, to go off to war in defiance of his father, and to commit a great sin against Eros by betraying Susannah. One wonders about Samuel's absence and the role it plays here. Tristan is the one who really sees into Susannah, really sees her, and that becomes a great story, because she reciprocates—she really understands Tristan as well. But she does not have him. On the other hand, Samuel has her promise, but he doesn't have her. And then, in the midst of all of these connections, comes the great scene—one of the best ever in film—when Alfred walks in just as Tristan is consoling Susannah. Alfred gets it all wrong, and sets into motion the unrelenting wheel of evil that is not satisfied until everyone has suffered intensely and is dead.

It is a great portrayal of the horror of jealousy and Aidan Quinn plays it superbly. Alfred's dark jealousy is set in motion at that moment; there is nothing more bloodthirsty than that scene. It is a modern *Othello*, Shakespeare's masterpiece about the same dark suspicion and Iago's great jealousy that got Othello to kill his beloved, and himself.

Susannah has been devastated by Samuel's decision to enlist, a decision he made without even telling her of his plans. Tristan is consoling her. Alfred walks in and gets it all wrong because of his jealousy. His accusation hangs in the air to bring ruin upon the whole family, and Alfred sets events in motion, things that he cannot ever take back.

We have looked now at Eros and feeling, and at feelings and emotions, as they begin to play out in this family, as the sons go off to war. The love story between Tristan and Susannah begins, with Alfred's jealousy seething in the background. We now turn to that unfolding of the myth—and to the love problem.

⚜ ⚜ ⚜ ⚜ ⚜ ⚜ ⚜ ⚜ ⚜

3

Love and Jealousy

Track 4,
To The
Boys

The love problem found in the great western myth of romantic love—*Tristan and Isolde*—now becomes the great story behind the unfolding of the plot and the future of the Ludlow family. Perhaps this modern retelling of the myth in *Legends of the Fall* can help us to understand something of the psychology behind it, and how to feel our way through its difficulties. We will take a closer look at love and jealousy, the anima and the animus, and the love triangle. (Here, too, are intimated stories of the Fall from Genesis: Eden, Cain and Abel, Jacob and Esau, the Tower of Babel—they're all here.)

When there is a triangle involved, we can be assured that things will not go well, and that some real suffering and pain lie ahead. It brings up the whole problem of being able to see and feel our way through these difficulties. We know that even in dogs, the number three changes the dynamics and they become a pack. In humans as well, the couple is caught up in rivalries, jealousies and collective patterns of behavior, which are destructive to all involved.

In order to approach the great myths in the right spirit, one must remember that there is a great tension about the meaning of words. Words can be just so much information. Jung tells us that words can lose their power; that they can get in the way of understanding. (CG Jung; *Letters* Vol.II) There is a great deal of difference between words spoken and the experience of being touched by what is behind the words. We want you to keep this difference in mind. This is particularly important in matters of the heart, which in our culture have been reduced to the trivial and the sentimental with very little discrimination for what we are actually talking about. A favorite image in all of our western religious tradition is Moses before the burning bush. Similarly, we think of the prophets, Isaiah and Ezekiel, who were admonished to be silent. As in these examples, one needs to put one's hand over one's mouth and be silent about something one could not possibly describe. Yet one has to try, because words are all we have. When given a distilled experience in words, hopefully the power of that experience will come through to touch you on a deeper level than that of just words. Jung said that when that happens, the Self could be constellated between writer and reader. The Self can convey what is behind the words.

Legends of the Fall heightens tension over words because it is a well-written story and because the music triggers feelings, memories and meaning. It has a quality about it that is splendid, magnificent, and sumptuous, and its quality is neither accidental nor contrived for filmmaking. Incidentally, it was good to read that Jim Harrison thought so, as well, upon seeing the film. It stands in stark contrast to all of the images of ugliness and superficiality and violence in our modern world. There is more than meets the eye in the line at the beginning when One Stab tells us that the Colonel went over the mountains "to lose the madness." He went over the mountains to lose the madness of war, the madness of the bureaucracy, and the madness of a country gone mad in its treatment of the Indians. We could add our own descriptions of the madness of the modern world—to lose the madness of the violence, the ugliness, the noise, the haste and the overcrowding. Then we could see clearly why everybody is starved to death for beauty, and why fantasies about nature are so common today. Nature in its beauty can be so appealing.

So the Colonel sought the majesty of the land and the beauty of the natural world—the wildlife and the splendid outdoors—to lose the madness. That is where he settled. Tristan carries all of that, as a warrior who honors the land and its wildlife. We notice something important in this film: finding that place and living there was not without suffering. In all good stories and in all good lives fully lived, there is a terrible amount of the horrific and the tragic even when surrounded by beauty. Yet the suffering is not meaningless or empty. Somehow in this story it is redemptive.

In this place the love problem comes to the fore, arriving with Samuel and Susannah from the East. We have already touched on how Samuel made a secret deal with his anima, leaving Susannah out of his decision to enlist in the war. It works both ways. Women also make deals with their animus, leaving the man out. Men make those secret deals a lot more often because men are not as close to Eros as women are. This may seem shocking and contradictory to everything that is popularly believed about men and women, and you may want to debate that statement. Allow me to demonstrate.

We have already looked at a man's dream about the father problem and how that has to be worked out by finding the way to carry both the father and the young, wild and creative energies. Now here is a woman's dream. Marie-Louise von Franz tells us that the dreamer was middle-aged, and that she had experienced deep love for a married man. He had reciprocated, but the dreamer had struggled with it for all the rational and conventional reasons. Here is her dream:

I heard the mighty and deep sound of a bronze bell. It was an extraordinary ringing I had never heard or seen before—a sound from beyond. It was of extraordinary beauty and irresistible. Fascinated, I got up, for I had to somehow get to the source of this sound, which could only be divine. Since the sound seemed sacred to me, I thought it would come from a church. Instantly I was in a church of the purest Gothic style of white stone. I was getting ready to climb the bell tower to find the bell—the source of this grave, rhythmic ringing, which I could still hear. But then everything changed. The church became a broad vault like the nave of a cathedral made of transparent, living, red-orange material, bathed in reddish light and supported by a forest of pillars that reminded me of stalactites in a cave that I had once seen in Spain. For a moment, I saw myself standing tiny and alone in this immense hall, dazzled with the sense that I had the whole world to explore. It was my heart. I was standing in the interior of my own heart. I realized at that moment that the wonderful sound that I could still hear was nothing more than the beating of my own heart, that the external sound and my heartbeat were one and the same. They were beating in the same rhythm. Macrocosm and microcosm were synchronized. The rhythm of the world's heart and my own heart were identical.

This powerful dream does not need much interpretation. While leaving the question of her dilemma up to the dreamer to decide, the dream was clearly saying that the woman was in a very holy place, the interior of her own heart. We have been talking about Eros, and Eros and the heart are inextricably bound together. (For a discussion in depth, refer to Hillman's *Jung's Typology.*) Women are closer to Eros; they are invested in Eros. The dream makes it very clear that the sound of the bell, the sound of her heart, was sacred to her, was sacred period.

Now imagine a big screen, something like a home movie screen or a big TV screen like one for the Super Bowl. That is our psyche. On the screen are main actors, affecting everything. There is the anima if you are a man or the animus if you are a woman. Those are the terms Jung used to describe the contra-sexual one in each of us. Then there is someone of the same sex as you, whom Jung calls *the shadow*. These actors operate behind the scenes in each one of us. Keep these actors in mind as we watch this film, *Legends of the Fall*. They are in the background of this story, clearly acting behind the scenes. If you can see how you project yourself as we talked about earlier, and see how these main actors operate in the background—you can see your own psyche. That is a major step in consciousness. You become aware of what is going on unconsciously behind the scenes and how to clean all that up.

When a man makes a deal with his anima—as Samuel does—and leaves the real woman out, any woman worth her salt is going to be outraged or devastated, or, at least, upset. She needs to be upset. She intuits that her man is more connected to something invisible (in this case, Samuel's feelings about the war) than to her. Her intuition is right. However, women too, can be more connected to something invisible—opinions, obligations (I "should," I "ought") or "preachers" (men with all the answers; men who patronize women)—than to the real man. Very often in life you have the untenable situation in which people are more connected to their invisible partners than to their visible ones. There are actual couples known in which the real marriage is with the anima and the animus and not with each other at all. That is what happened in the marriage between the Colonel and Isabel. They were not married at all. As Tristan says, "They loved mostly the idea of each other." Perhaps we all know couples like that.

What is the anima? The anima is all of a man's fantasies about women—how women should be. The real woman gets to carry all of that for him, unfortunately. The anima is all that a man finds desirable, a system of expectations operating unconsciously in his relationships and judgments with a woman in this case. The anima is an erotic relationship fantasy.

If outer expectations—such as ordinary sex, or schemes of power or money—get tangled up with the anima or the animus, everything could be messed up, and everything could be lost. The conscious recognition of the anima or the animus means loving the other person for herself or himself, as well as for love's sake, not one's own ideas about love. Conscious recognition of the anima or the animus will help to remove those two creatures so that the real person can be loved for who he/she is and for love's sake. When one follows conscious love, then real love is fulfilled.

However, the anima is also able to become a source of inspiration and fantasy, the source of a melody, the source of creativity. She is inside so she enlivens the man from within. In the romantic American imagination, there is the misguided notion that my love is supposed to follow me and fulfill me. No. It is the other way around. The first is an egocentric notion, and it does not serve the soul. It is just the opposite. Only for the man who pursues the anima for her own sake—that is, the sake of his soul—does she become Beatrice as she did for Dante in *The Divine Comedy*.

Similarly, the animus can do the same for a woman. For the animus insight is what counts, a truth for truth's sake. Then a woman's truth can stand up to any mixture of sensuality, power, craving, or jealously. Only a woman who loves truth for its own sake will be able to integrate the animus. The animus then becomes—like the anima—a bridge to the Self, a source of creativity and inspiration. Then she will notice that while she is doing her make-up, or otherwise engaged in ordinary activities, she will get an idea or see an image that has a strange power to it. That is the animus, and it is just about as magical as that. In just that way, the animus provides a bridge to the unconscious and it can be the source of inspiration and creativity for a woman when it is integrated.

Many women ask, "When will I get there? When will the animus become a positive creative energy in my life?" The answer is only when she can get the negative, unrelated, ugly one out of the way, and into a bottle with a cork in it. She has to stop being so connected to her ideas of how men—and relationships—should be and deal with the real man in her life, her real relationship, and real situation. A woman must either bail out or get off the fence. She must do something and not sit around philosophizing about how "they are" or how 'my husband is always disappointing me.' Otherwise, she runs the risk of the provisional life in her relationships.

When the invisible partners prevail, the two flesh and blood people flounder. They flounder because the woman is more connected to her inner idea of how a man and a woman should be, and the man is more connected to his feeling of how women are supposed to be. Both have unrealistic expectations and both are unrelated to their actual partner. That is why Jack Sanford entitled his bestselling book, *The Invisible Partners*. It is a "must read" masterful description of how these two invisible partners get in the way. You have to get them out of the way or they will mess everything up. They do not belong "out there" or in the middle of your relationships. They belong on the inside, giving you creative images.

When the invisible partners are not integrated and when they are operating unconsciously, the two flesh and blood people flounder because they keep coming up against something else, something they don't understand. For example, one evening the man gets up from the dinner table and suddenly, he's in a mood. She is mystified. She wonders, "What the hell happened? He was just eating supper and everything was fine. Now look at him. He is over there in a snit." Conversely, the woman may change just as inexplicably. One minute she is warm and related, and then suddenly she is distant and cold as a cucumber. The man scratches his head, and then what most men usually do next is to throw their hands up in dismay and walk out of the room—or the marriage. Or they will use whatever avenue is handy to get away. Men are not noted for hanging around emotional scenes. In both cases of the man and woman—perhaps in all cases—something invisible has happened, usually in the feeling realm. Some feeling has not been expressed. In the movie, for example, Samuel has not told Susannah of his feeling about the war, of his plans to enlist. "Oh, Susannah, I meant to tell you tonight."

Lurking between the two, waiting to mess things up, is Mr. or Ms.

Dark Person, the Shadow. It is lurking behind the scenes ready to fill in and to jump into the vacuum when feelings are not expressed. So when Samuel announces he is off to enlist, Susannah walks away distraught, devastated. Here then, is a great opportunity for feelings. She can feel hurt or she can feel disappointed. Or she can feel crushed. Even those negative feelings are OK, because those are all healthy, feeling reactions. But what if there is a "little twist" and she feels victimized by this man who "always" takes advantage of her? Then, the feeling has turned dark and a complex is activated. She identifies with being an innocent, helpless victim, and her self-pity and resentment begin to build with poison from the animus. At this point, a little detective work would be able to find the animus, which uses words like "always" and "never" to add more resentment to the mix. It takes detective work to find these characters—the anima, the animus, and the shadow—but it's not really very hard, because if you are honest, they are very disturbing. By the time the anima or the animus has finished adding its poison to the mix, your feeling has been jarred, the shadow has jumped in, and no one knows what is going to happen next. It rocks a person's world. One either feels enraged, or filled with despair, or jealous, or lustful, or passionate. Whatever it is, one now has the burr under his saddle. He feels he just can't sit there anymore and take this. Interestingly enough, if the person will just sit there with it, he can hopefully begin to regain some composure and realize he is "beside himself." He will then get the clue that "something is going on with his screen, the psyche, and he needs to see the actors operating behind this scene. He needs to clear up his psychic screen."

The more we pay attention to our reactions, the more we clean up our screens, the better off we are. Then things will begin to go better for us. This clarification is often called "coming home" because that is how clarity feels. It feels like coming home to one's self. This process is really becoming, and it is really enjoyable. It makes you feel more centered, more solid, more harmonious, and less restless; less scared, and less like the ground is falling out from under you. One is becoming one with one's self—there is no longer psychic interference.

What do we have to do to get there? We have to pull all of the stuff we project out there, and get it back here, where it belongs. That is why young people—like the young people in the Ludlow family—have so much to grow into. Furthermore, isn't that a wonderful view of life and what life is all about—growing into our selves?

Now with all this in mind, let us to return to some scenes from the movie. Susannah has arrived, and this is the first meal at the homestead, with the father, the three brothers, and the new lady, Susannah. First we see the men, all formally dressed for dinner, standing around the table. The Colonel asks the blessing, while the boys engage in quiet jokes and horseplay, and then all are seated.

> Alfred: [To Samuel] Tell father what you were saying about Vienna.
> Colonel: Samuel, what's that?
> Samuel: Oh, it's the Kaiser. He won't lift a finger to stop them from annihilating Serbia.
> Colonel: Let's not talk about war at the table, please.
> Samuel: Well Susannah hears that all England is mobilizing.
> Colonel: Ah.
> Samuel: Well, we're stuck out here in the middle of nowhere while all of this is going on.
> Colonel: Thank God for that.
> Samuel: Well you wouldn't want us to evade our duty.
> Colonel: Wouldn't I?
> Samuel: Father, with all due respect—
> Susannah [enters the room:] Excuse me, but everything is packed so carefully, I couldn't find anything.
> [All the men stand, and remain standing until she is seated]
> Susannah: Thank you. [She giggles at their attentiveness. The men then begin to all pass food to her, awkwardly and competitively.] Thank you. [She laughs.]

After dinner, Samuel is singing to Susannah's accompaniment on the piano.

> "As evening fell, a maiden stood at the edge of a wood.
> In her hands lay the reins of a stallion.
> And ne'er I see a girl as fair, or a gentler horse anywhere.
> Whisper alas, "She belonged, she belonged to another. Another.
> Forever.
> Yes, she belonged to the twilight and the mist."

The Colonel writes to Isabel:
Dear Isabel,
How strange to have a cultivated woman in the house again. And how intoxicating. Indeed, to have all three of my sons under my roof again fills me with such a deep quiet sense of satisfaction that I thank God.

That is the Ludlow family now with the arrival of Susannah. Notice what happened when Susannah came into the room. The men are all there, talking about the war, and when Susannah walks in, they start falling all over each other. You can get the feeling right there of Susannah's filling in the gap, the absent feminine—or as the Colonel writes, "How strange to have a woman in the house again." As a friend said to me recently, "Just add a woman, and everything changes"—and not always for the better, as we see in this film. But it does change, and it is alive. A real woman always has an effect on men, conscious or unconscious.

The second thing to notice is Samuel's song—his strange little duet with Susannah. Here are all of these rugged rough men, and then here is this sweet little duet, which doesn't seem quite appropriate in the setting. Did you notice what all the men are doing? They are captivated by their anima fantasies, aren't they? They look at Susannah, and then they are just "going to town" with their fantasies—a wonderful example of anima projection. Listen to the words of Samuel's song—"Ne'er have I seen such a fair maiden; one who has been given to another." That is interesting in light of future developments and especially since Samuel sings it, the brother to whom she is supposed to belong. This scene reminds one of Shakespeare's line, "Ne'er a faint heart a woman did win." This is about love, which you do not win with a faint heart.

The contrasts in this scene are striking. Take a moment to compare Samuel with Siegfried—the hero in Wagner's opera of that name. Brünhilde is the maiden sought by Siegfried, and it is she who eventually teaches him healthy fear. The dragon couldn't teach him to fear, the evil dwarfs couldn't, hell and fire and brimstone couldn't, but Brünhilde, the woman, could. Only a real woman can teach a certain fear to a man. In the story of the opera, Brünhilde is cast into a trance and surrounded by a ring of fire, set by her father. Only the man who is brave enough to get through the fire wins Brünhilde.

This is always true in love. You have to be brave enough and struggle enough to win such a person of extraordinary beauty and irresistibility.

Love is not just what makes the world go around. It is also what moves the psyche. One has to be willing to take on that ring of fire, which was set by Wotan, the father of Brünhilde. So you have to kill the father, and you have to go against the old; you have to go against your fears. That is what it takes to rescue the one you love. That is the masculine role. What about the feminine? It is also important for women who are encased in that kind of ring of fire to face their fears as well, and put the fire out, even if it means facing Beelzebub himself, to get out of their trance. So for both men and women, it is important to face the fire and go through it, even though for Brünhilde it is primarily to receive Siegfried.

Next we notice the Colonel's words in his letter to Isabel—"How strange and how intoxicating" to have a woman around the house again. To put that in Jungian terms, "How intoxicating it is to be around the anima. How intoxicating it is to have the feel of the feminine, a feminine atmosphere."

Intoxication, however, is not the best way to deal with her, as the brothers find out and as Susannah herself finds out. This poor woman walks into what can only be described as heaven, if you are starved for men, or hell, if you find yourself being ogled by four men, because she becomes the anima woman for all of them. First of all, she is beautiful. That always helps—or hurts—depending on your point of view. When the woman is beautiful, then men can project all sorts of goddess qualities onto her. Beautiful women easily catch projections. In fact, sometimes it can be a curse (Jung's term.) In the movie, she wears white clothes all of the time, which makes her look very fresh, and virginal, and innocent—although we get some strong hints that she is not innocent at all. She becomes, in the language of Jung, the classic anima woman. She carries the anima for all of them, which means that she is expected to live out what they expect. That expectation is a very impossible role for any flesh-and-blood woman. Thus, beauty becomes the cause of many feminine wars, as opposed to aggression-caused masculine wars.

Marilyn Monroe was one of the classic anima women of all time along with Cleopatra, Beatrice, and Carmen. She constellated the anima for thousands, perhaps even millions of men. If a woman does not own herself, if she does not know and does not own her own individual nature, she becomes a blank screen on which men project their fantasies, and the screen says "Put on me whatever you want and I will be it. I will smile, and I will be pleasing." (It can happen even if a woman does own herself, but she will quickly object.)

What does Susannah do as she begins to live among these men? She learns to shoot, to ride, and to rope—she learns to do everything the guys do on the ranch. She becomes pleasing. The anima woman becomes psychologically pleasing to the masculine element nearest her, and Susannah learns to do everything expected of her. She fits right in. She pleases them, and in the process—except for a few hints here and there about her ideas and her passion—we really don't know much about Susannah at all, except for her beauty. What is it about her beauty that is so captivating? It is so fresh. She has a lovely energy, a fresh face, and a wonderful smile. She has a gentle, teasing spirit that is very feminine, and it attracts all of that projection. All of the men are taken with her.

That does not mean that a woman shouldn't be any of those things. But beyond her attractive persona, we really don't know who Susannah is. Certainly that doesn't work very well for women today. Consciousness has changed for the feminine, and a woman cannot very well get away with being an anima woman, because somewhere inside of her is a demand that she also be herself. To be herself means that very soon she will have to say "no" to a man, and that she won't be what he wants in some situation. That brings real trouble, because that is not the way the anima is supposed to play. That is not the fantasy most men have. Most men have the fantasy—and it is the biggest fantasy of all—of wafting away in the eternal feminine, where everything is OK. "You smile, you please me, you bring me my supper, you fix my clothes, and you don't give me any grief." That is the anima fantasy most men have. The alchemists called it "Solutio" where men become liquid—messy instead of solid. "Solutio" literally means turning a solid into liquid.

At times we do get glimpses that Susannah is a real woman. In those moments, she knows more than all the rest of them put together. For example, there is the scene with little Isabel (Isabel Two), when Susannah laughs at the men—when she makes fun of the father and Alfred, and their rivalry for another woman. In that same scene we learn that Isabel Two, who is only thirteen, has already picked Tristan as the one whom she will marry. The men do not see these things. They are unaware of these women as they really are, and it is upon their blank screens that they project. It is upon that blank screen that Alfred projects his own dark jealousy. But Isabel Two already knows her destiny. And, as it turns out, she knows correctly. Jung would call that the "natural mind of a woman."

Before we get to that, there is the scene where the sons confront their father about the war. We have talked about this scene before in terms of the relationship of the father to his sons. This time, we revisit the scene in more detail and I want you to notice the Colonel and his integration of the anima, in contrast to Samuel.

[The family is gathered in the house. The Colonel is reading aloud from Rudyard Kipling, while Samuel reads the newspaper. Samuel suddenly throws the paper down in disgust, and jumps up, pacing the room restlessly.]

> The Colonel: I could read another story you know, Sam.
> Samuel: [Exasperated] The Germans broke through at Armentieres.
> Alfred: What?
> Samuel: The entire British third corps is trapped in the Belgian lowlands…and this paper is already a week old!
> The Colonel: Calm Down.
> Samuel: Father, with my fluent German, I could become an officer.
> The Colonel: Yes, and lead other young boys to the slaughter, and be slaughtered yourself.
> Samuel: The men who served under you worshipped you.
> The Colonel: And they were damn fools, all of them, weren't they?
> Samuel: This is a turning point in the history of the world. How can you—
> The Colonel: How can I what?
> Alfred: Father, you can't expect us not to be a part of this. You taught us—
> The Colonel: I taught you to think for yourselves, that's what I taught you.
> Samuel: And to defend what is ours.

The Colonel: Yes! What is ours. What is ours!
Alfred: Well, we have already lost two of our cousins at the Marne.
The Colonel: Whom we have never even met. And don't talk to me boys, as though I have never seen a war!

Can the reader see clearly that the Colonel is not related to his anima in any phony way? Every time these young mavericks try to sentimentalize something or to present half-truths, he cuts right through their sentiment. He says, "It's not that." "No!" "It's not that." "Don't confuse it, boys. Don't get mushy." You see, the anima will do that; the anima will sentimentalize and mush everything up. The anima mixes levels and feelings. "We've lost two cousins already!" they protest. But they don't even know these cousins, and the Colonel steps in to say, "Don't tell me about heart wrench." To be able to do that is an act of logos and discrimination, and can be of great service to clarity.

In this encounter, you heard the best description of projection in the Colonel's words. The son said to him, "But father, all the men who served under you worshipped you." And the Colonel answered, "And they were damn fools, weren't they?" He cut right through the inflation. *To worship someone is dangerous psychologically—it is dangerous in all cases.*

Samuel will not be deterred however, and the argument continues. Samuel points out that this is the war to end all wars, that his father never saw a war like this one:

The Colonel: They said that about the War of Secession. That's what they said about the Indian Wars. That is what people who sell newspapers say about wars.
Samuel: This is not the Indian Wars. We're fighting against naked aggression.
The Colonel: There will be no more talk of wars in this house! Damn it!

[An awkward silence follows, and Susannah enters the room. The Colonel invites her to sit down.]

Samuel: [facing his father] I am going to Canada to enlist.
{Susannah is stunned.]
Alfred: And I'm going with him.
[The Colonel walks out of the room.]

Samuel: [to Susannah] I'm sorry, my love. I meant to speak to you tonight. I know you'll understand—it's the only honorable thing to do.

[Susannah is devastated. She leaves the room. She seeks out Tristan, who is opening up a book, and finding a map.]

Susannah: What is that?
Tristan: It's a book my father wrote to get the government to change its policies toward the Indians in the Dakotas.
Susannah: Samuel won't change his mind.
Tristan: Change it for him. [That is right to the point. But the anima woman, Susannah, shyly backs away—that would mean losing her vagueness. She turns and looks at the picture of the Colonel and Isabel.]
Susannah: What happened between them?
Tristan: Mother said she never liked it here. I think they loved mostly the idea of each other.
Susannah: [Breaks down. Tristan holds her.] Please don't let him go.
Tristan: Shh. Shh. [Comforts her.] I'll take care of him. Shh.

[Alfred enters the room, and sees Tristan holding Susannah. His eyes darken as he stares at them. Susannah turns away. Tristan walks right by Alfred and leaves the room.]

The Colonel writes to Isabel:
October 14, 1914
Dear Isabel,
Today our sons are leaving home to defend an England they have never seen, and I am unable to stop them. Ah, Isabel. I have tried to shelter our sons from all the madness, and now they go to seek it.

[It is the next morning. The household is gathered in the yard to send the boys off to the war. The Colonel has asked One Stab to escort the boys to Canada and to bring back the horses. Susannah is devastated and lost as she tells Samuel goodbye. Then the Colonel comes outside, and calls his sons, one by one.]

> Colonel: Alfred. [Alfred steps forward and shakes his father's hand, then embraces him.]
> Alfred: Goodbye. Don't worry, father.
> The Colonel: Take care now. [Alfred steps back.] Samuel. [Samuel steps forward confidently.]
> Samuel: I'll bring you back the Kaiser's helmet.
> The Colonel: Bring yourself back. That would please me more. [He embraces Samuel. Then he calls for Tristan.] Tristan. Take care of Samuel. [Tristan gives his word, embraces his father.]
> Tristan: I will.

[The boys mount up and leave, the household watches, grieving.]

Now the boys leave for the war. It would be hard to find a more profoundly moving scene than this one. Samuel is inflated; he has a positive inflation—"I'll bring back the Kaiser's helmet"—but the Colonel cuts right through the inflation and replies, "Just bring yourself back." This is an enormous triumph of masculinity in that scene. It takes enormous ego strength to do what the Colonel did— he hated everything they were doing, yet he sent them off, with his best horses, and with One Stab as escort. That takes tremendous strength. No nice phrases. No sugary stuff. No polite small talk. The Colonel cuts right through it.

It is a great act of ego strength for a man and for a father to be able to do that—to face his adversaries, who are doing what he doesn't want them to do, and to let them go anyway. What proves even greater ego strength is that he does it actively. He could have stayed in his room, pouting. He could have thrown a fit and kicked them out of the house. He could have had all sorts of angry or anima-mood responses, but he didn't. He pulled all that emotion and all that feeling into himself. He went out into the yard anyway and faced them, calling each by name and then he sent them away to a war he hated. For our concerns, this scene deserves a psychological

Academy Award. It is a masterpiece of father-love, and father-relatedness. It is so understated that it is brilliant.

How different from our current culture's treatment of fathers. Current fathers are not very honored. Either they carry the opposites of "stupidity" and are the butt of jokes, as on current TV, or they are the harsh tyrants of violence.

It seems anticlimactic after that magnificent scene, to change our focus to the shadow, and to the problem of jealousy. Actually it is symbolically accurate, because that is precisely what jealousy does. It fouls up the entire scene. Alfred's dark jealousy wreaks havoc upon this family. Jealousy is in his dark look at Susannah and Tristan, and that jealousy unfolds in the rest of the film.

One of the best books I know on the subject of jealousy is called *Cinderella and her Sisters—The Envied and The Envying*. Another good place to read about jealousy is in *She* by Robert Johnson, in which he talks about the jealousy of Psyche's sisters in the Psyche-Amor myth. *Cinderella* is the classic story, of course. You can be sure that every time one gets the glass slipper, there will be jealous sisters—or witches—around to spoil the party. As von Franz illustrates so eloquently and brilliantly over and over again, but especially in her classic work of Jungian literature, *Puer Aeternus*, it is the witch mother who would steal life itself that she is jealous of. The negative mother complex at her most lethal is the mother who hates the life of her offspring. She does not want them to live, even as she says it in the name of life. (For example, the over-anxious mother.)

A woman would be really stupid if she allowed the witch mother to intrude. Men as well.

We know that Alfred really loves Susannah himself, which would be O.K., if he could admit it and struggle with it. But he doesn't. And so his jealousy eventually drives him away from the rest of the family, into politics and eventually into collusion with the Irish mafia. That sets up the rivalry between his family and the Irish mafia over the illegal importation and distribution of whiskey in the era of prohibition—the business of bootlegging, which Tristan has taken up to earn back the family's fortunes. In a confrontation between Tristan and the Irish bullies, Isabel Two—by now Tristan's wife and the mother of his two children—is fatally shot. This in turn leads to Susannah's suicide. Finally, there is the scene of confrontation between the family and the mob, which intends to wipe out the Ludlow rivalry once and for all. Alfred's jealousy had wheels. In a wonderful twist of irony, it also proved the fitting moment for Alfred to redeem himself. Only in the final scene does he redeem himself from the rules when he intervenes, shooting his father's and Tristan's enemies—the police who had been sent and paid off by the mob. His redemption comes but not before he has lost everything, including the one he never had, Susannah. If you think jealousy is a minor vice, you need to know that it can be this dark. You need to see this movie.

Let us take a closer look at jealousy. In general, the people who have not tended to themselves are most liable to jealousy. It is only when we look around that we find things to be jealous of, because if you are fully occupied with your life, and your plate is full, there is no time to be jealous of anything or anyone. Jealousy is most likely to take place when "a portion of your plate is vacant." However, jealousy is one of the great schemes that life and the devil have to get you into life; that way is to get you thoroughly jealous. Jealousy is the great "projection getter." I repeat: *jealousy is a projection getter, or a great hook*. Jealousy is a projection about the qualities we have not developed, or about those we have not enriched in ourselves. We are jealous of some aspect that we need to develop in our own lives. It then becomes easy to see that the twin sister of jealousy is laziness.

If you do not tend to your own self, and develop your own life, it is possibly because of laziness. There is always a laziness hanging around which does not want to do the work of tending to yourself. That laziness would much rather hang around and be jealous of what the other person has accomplished. "You can see it." "It is all done." "It's beautiful." "Cinderella has already got the slipper on." "I would have to go to work on my own slipper." That is why laziness is labeled jealousy's twin sister.

Listen to this story about a friend who worked with analyst Jack Sanford. Sanford had just published his book, *Healing and Wholeness,* and the young man thought that book was just the "cat's meow"—it was wonderful. The gist of the book was also what the friend had been thinking about in the back of his head, and he told Sanford so. He said, "I am very jealous of your book. It is so damn good." Without skipping a beat, Sanford shot right back at him, "Oh, well, that's a good sign because it means you have it in you." Right then and there he turned the friend's jealousy into a sour pickle. It is a sour pickle to have to own what belongs to you. Sanford stopped him right in his tracks and made the young man own that he had it in himself to develop his own writing skills. From that perspective, jealousy is a good sign, because it means that whatever you are jealous of, you have within yourself. Take heart the next time you scout around, and you feel that worm of jealousy take hold of you; whatever it is you are jealous of, you have within yourself.

The classic tale of *Cinderella* and her jealous stepsisters is so appropriate in the talk about jealousy, because it is usually some aspect of the feminine not honored within us that is at the root of it. If you find yourself in the middle of such a fire, it is helpful to remember that evil wants to burn itself up in the end. You have to stoke your jealousy for all its worth—no censorship is allowed. No throwing water over it to put it out. Own your jealousy. Tend to it it, let it burn, and let nature take its course, if you can stand it. It takes ego strength to be able to stand that fiery jealousy and not want to hurt the other, which is the natural response. You have to own that too—otherwise the ugly sister goes underground and bites you in the rear end. To want to get back at the one who has hurt you is natural. It is not the best of nature, but it is natural. If you own that in yourself, you can speak to it. If you don't own it, you will spread the fire, or you will spread evil. It is much better to own it, stoke it, and just let the fire burn itself out. On the other hand, if you really hate someone, let him or her have whatever it is they seek, or whatever it is you want to deny them. It will either burn him up, or he might show you something in return, which will make you deal with your hatred for a second time. But if you try to fight him directly, you will only get scorched. You cannot fight fire with fire.

In other words, let the other person be burned in the fires of his own greed. If you know somebody who is really ambitious, who is stepping all over your toes, and aggravating the hell out of you, your natural tendency is to want to strangle them, or kill them or whatever. If you back off, back away, and let them have what they seek, you will see the drama unfold, and you will be amazed. Ninety-nine per cent of the time, there is no worse punishment because the chances are that what they seek does not belong to them anyway, and the result will burn them up. It is just a greedy little libido fire, which burns itself up. People are burned up by their own greed, so it is wise not to interfere.

Jealousy is greedy libido. We all have areas of greedy libido like Alfred. We need to check up on the Alfred in ourselves. You can plainly see there is a beautiful woman there, and you know that it is pretty natural to fall for her—there's nobody else around for a hundred miles, and it is pretty damn healthy to fall in love with her. It isn't healthy to deny that, to let it all go underground. Allowed to go underground, it will do some of those terrorist activities, just like it did with Alfred. You can count on it. We all have areas of greedy libido. It is a fire that will burn itself up and it is wise to remember that. It is very wise when you encounter a greedy person or a jealous person, an angry person or a crazy person, or a lusty person—allow them to have their meanness. Do not get in their way because you will hold back God who is trying to give them a good singe. You will only get in the way. That is especially true if it is your family—mothers with children, for instance. The children have to learn about their greedy libido too. You must not interfere with anyone, unless it is with a very good friend, and even then, only maybe.

You must bring consciousness into the situation. Jung says that it is always good when you see a dragon to remind him that you know that he is already doomed. The dragon is already doomed because he has to eat himself up. You must say it to a dragon, which means you must be conscious enough to see the dragon. By giving other people enough rope, as the saying goes, they hang themselves. If you give the other person enough rope or power, his own power eats him and you can step out of the way. The frantic little ego has its own agenda. It does not want to get out of the way. It wants to get in there and be God, and it urges you to retaliate or seek revenge. If you do, you will get caught in the fire.

That brings up the last question—what if it is you? What if it is your libido, your fire, your jealousy, and your meanness? You must face your own evil, your own greed. If you are an Alfred, you must own your own desire and lust, or your love and affection. Because if you don't own it, the shadow will get it. A person's shadow as a rule has to do with greed of some kind. The shadow is a greedy thing.

There is another issue here—the issue of possessiveness. Much of the time the quest for what we call love is really about a quest for power. Alfred wants to have Susannah, no matter what.

Had he been able to sacrifice his ego need to have her, our story would have had a different caste. Was it his love for her or was it his need for power? Very often in relationships, the right and wrong motives are mixed up and the involvement becomes a battle between love and power, said Marie Louise von Franz in an interview in *Psychological Perspectives* in 1987. The inability to give up personal power when it is appropriate is a major block on the path to growth. If we have spent a long time acting like saints, we might think we do not have any greed or power drive. The truth may come as a great shock to us. We might get indigestion and migraine headaches. But if we own it, then it will burn itself up and transform us. It cannot do that if we don't see it. If we own our greed and power, we see it and know it. If we know there is a fire burning in us, we can put ours in the container and watch it. Watch it: do not judge it, panic or say, "I shouldn't feel like this." Just watch it, and have the courage to feel it, and let it burn. Thus you will learn a great deal about your soul and about yourself in the process.

Tend to your jealousy and your fire—your anger, your meanness and your Alfred. Ultimately, that awareness will help you to earn your soul, and the Self will be pleased. Then you will have the courage, like the Colonel, to do the great thing.

⚜ ⚜ ⚜ ⚜ ⚜ ⚜ ⚜ ⚜ ⚜

4

Tristan: A Knight's Tale

Track 1, Legends;
Track 7, Descent Into Madness

The story of Tristan is archetypal, which means that Tristan can become a mythic figure with his story portraying a particular pattern in human life—in this case, the transformation and redemption of the hero. We need these stories, these myths. They show us things we need to see. They can teach us so much about what it means to be human, and what it means to be heroic. The archetype of the hero is well documented in Joseph Campbell's book, *The Hero with a Thousand Faces*. We have already alluded to the fact that Tristan's name is fascinating and an interesting choice because he is a particular type of hero connected to the great Western romantic myth, *Tristan and Isolde*. That myth came from Cornwall, in England, the same place Colonel Ludlow came from, and it originated during the Middle Ages, in the era of the stories of the great knights. Another synchronicity. So, we can say that Tristan's story is a knight's tale, a story of the transformation and redemption of the hero in the Western European tradition of romance.

The word "romance" comes from the knight's tales of the Middle Ages in France, *Les Romans Courtois*. These tales—originally based on the *Chansons de geste,* or songs of high deeds—were first sung by the troubadours, and then written down. In written form, they became long novels (or *"romans"* in French) written in verse, usually in rhymed couplets. As "noble" literature, they were written for the entertainment of the court, the nobility.

Of these *romans courtois,* the most famous in French literature is that of *Tristan and Isolde*. It is among the oldest and most well-known literature of the Middle Ages. Like the stories of King Arthur and the Knights of the Round Table, the material for *Tristan and Isolde* was based on Celtic legends from Cornwall. It is a prototype, the first literature of its kind, and a knight's tale of adventure undertaken in honor of his lady. We need to recognize that before the Middle Ages, this sense of romance, or romantic adventure, did not exist; we often forget this fact. In these gallant, wondrous stories of the knights, who was his lady, the damsel the knight wanted to champion and impress? Usually it was not the lady to whom he was married. In this sense, that was the beginning of romance outside of marriage.

When we look at this word "romance," we discover that romance was not at all what we usually think of today. It was a fictitious tale. Romance began with a fictitious tale of wondrous events, with much imagination and high adventure for the knight. Only much later does it become the material of novels where the emphasis is on love. Love is a word so terribly misused in the English language we ought to throw it out. It means too many things with so much sentimental baggage attached to it, that we don't have any idea what it really means. If you associate love with romance, you might be interested to know that one of the dictionary's definitions of romance is "an exaggeration or fabrication that has no real substance."

The question becomes how do we sort out this confusion between love and romance? Here again, we have to make very clear distinctions between real feeling, real emotions, and romance. Real feeling is very different from sentiment, or sentimentality, or sweetness. Sometimes men become "crazy" because women get stuck in sentiment, and never go farther into the real feeling. But men get stuck in sentiment also. It takes real reflection to know the difference between sentiment and real feeling. Both men and women alike need to get beyond sentiment and into real feeling, which is the hard work of valuing.

The story of Tristan is a knight's tale in the real sense of that word. It is a tale of redemption, in which all is given for "my lady," for the feminine. We know that "my lady" means "my soul"—it is everything "for my soul" that we do. It is also a tale of the knight's redemption, which comes through the father, the Colonel, who continues to carry so much life and clarifying energy throughout the film. We have seen that the gift of the masculine is the ability to cut through the phony, the sentimental, the arid distractions, and the projections—what the film calls "to lose the madness"—without crushing the person. Everyone needs that ability. Anthony Hopkins' portrayal of the father shows that kind of masculine strength again and again, though it is not always loved. As we learn in the film, redemption does not come without suffering, without pain; it is the Fall.

Legends of the Fall is so lush with beauty, music and feeling because it is the container for all of that pain. One has to have such a rich container to be able to carry so much. The film portrays all that goes wrong in our lives. It is not just about Tristan—it is about all of us. The transformation that Tristan undergoes is archetypal, and it must be taken in that way. We must not take it personally because we would find it far too oppressive. On one hand, do not be afraid to notice where the story touches you, but on the other, remember it is archetypal. It is about all of "humankind," not just about one person. There are some incredibly oppressive scenes in this film.

The first scene begins with the war; it is one of the most brutal portrayals of the horrors of war, ever. Let us return to the film now to see the tale of Tristan unfold.

> *One Stab narrates: "The Colonel told me, ride with them to Calgary, and bring back the horses. "Damn fools," he called them. "Damn fools." The Colonel would not have them ride off to war on old nags, damn fools or not."*

Through Samuel's letters to Susannah, we are introduced to the horrors of the war, and the loss of some of his idealism. Samuel now realizes he was "naïve." Still he seeks to distinguish himself in battle, and remains assured of God's favor against the enemy. We see all three brothers engaged in a terrifically fierce artillery battle, probably with chemical warfare. Samuel is slightly grazed as Tristan dives and pulls him into a foxhole, and Alfred takes shrapnel in the leg. The battlefield is littered with corpses.

In the next scene, on the way to visiting Alfred in the field hospital, Samuel is called aside to translate some intercepted German messages. When another man returns from the front wounded, Samuel volunteers to replace him. Tristan and Alfred learn that Samuel has gone to the front lines without Tristan. Tristan mounts his horse, riding frantically in search of his brother, who has been caught in an ambush.

Tristan: Samuel! Samuel!

Track 5, Samuel's Death

His horse falls from under him, and he continues on foot, turning over the dead soldiers as he goes on, looking for Samuel. We see Samuel, in a foxhole on the front lines, his buddy now a corpse, and he begins running—not toward safety, but toward the barbed wire fence. He is blinded by the explosions of poisonous gas and his panic, unable to see, his eyes chemically ruined, while Tristan is trying to find him among all the smoke, the exploding gaseous artillery shells, the dead, the dying men and horses. Samuel repeatedly calls for Tristan to help him, but before Tristan can reach him, Samuel is mortally wounded, caught in the barbed wire stretched across the front lines from which he is unable to free himself.

Tristan: [Seeing his brother caught, then ripped apart by machine-gun fire] N-O-O-O-O! I got you. I got you. You're doing good. We're going home. Damn it, Samuel. Samuel. Samuel? [Samuel has died.] Oh no. Oh no! No! No! God damn you, God. Ah. Goddamn God.

What a moment. Damning God. Shocking, but absolutely real. It reminds one literally of Jung's *Answer to Job,* where Jung describes at length and with Tristan's rage, the dark side of God. And how, if we are honest, we have all been to that dark place where life seems totally senseless, where we are angry with God and for what He has done.

Psychologically, it is a very dark place for the personality and why all major religions warn against it—but, now, in this new age, they do so with fossilizing effects.

This is the great blow to the knight, the knight who has been used to wrestling with the bear and winning. He doesn't win here. Remember his vow, his honor. He had given his word to his father that he would take care of Samuel. But Samuel went to the front lines without him, and because of that, Tristan was unable to keep his promise. Here we might note that we have all been in the place where we want to scream "N-O-O-O" like Tristan, to the horrors of life. Still, it is important for the hero—and the heroic in each of us—to go through the panic and tragedy anyway. Jung wrote: "For the hero fear is a challenge and a task because only boldness can deliver from fear. And if the challenge is not taken, the meaning of life is somehow violated and the whole future is condemned to hopeless staleness, to a drab grey, lit only by will-o'-the wisps." (CW5, pp 551)

And perhaps the fear of evil is the greatest fear there is.

George Bernard Shaw wrote:

"If a person cannot look evil in the face without illusion, he will never know what it really is or combat it effectively. The few people who have been able relatively to do this have been called cynics, and have sometimes had an abnormal share of evil in themselves, corresponding to the abnormal strength of their minds, but they have never done mischief unless they intended to do it. That is why great scoundrels have been beneficent rulers while amiable and perfectly harmless leaders have ruined their countries by trusting to the hocus pocus of innocence and guilt, instead of facing up to the facts without either malice or evil." (Shaw, *Major Barbara*)

That is a description of the journey for modern man. Jung said that the number one problem of the modern world is dealing with evil—especially your own. Only if you have dealt with your own evil, can you look evil in the face. Seeing Samuel caught on the barbed wire, his body torn apart by bullets and gas, wrecks Tristan, and he screams out that cry—"N-O-O-O-O"—at the horror of that sight. It is almost incomprehensible to him. He is wrecked. He screams out his agony and his rage. But then he has to go on. He now performs the ritual of the hunter, the ritual of setting his brother's spirit free. He takes out his knife, and just as One Stab has taught him, he cuts out his brother's heart, and holds it in his hands.

This is a real funeral ritual, full of power. In the movie, notice the faces of the soldiers as he returns. They feel the primal, raw power of Tristan's actions and his sorrow. War is a terrible thing. His fellow soldiers feel that power, and they feel his connection to the primitive hunter within himself, the warrior. (If one owns the video, it might be good to watch this scene again.)

Then we see One Stab at home, awakened in his sleep at the same time, as if from a powerful dream. Once more, we are made aware of the psychic connection between One Stab and Tristan. It is the most telling ritual of a funeral one can see.

The war has taken its toll. Tristan is overcome by the madness of war and he is discharged. (Incidentally, many of the scenes of Tristan's madness were deleted in the film.) Samuel has died. Alfred comes home wounded and lame. Tristan does not go home. He sends word that he cannot return. He tells them he will send Samuel's heart home but that he has gone to sea. We are reminded of Sir Laurens van der Post, who also could not return home after the Second World War. He too went into seclusion, to recover from the madness of war. (As well as to not "infect" his family, cf. the video, *All Africa Within Us*.)

Looked at in this way, we can see the wisdom of both Tristan and van der Post. One cannot simply return to so-called "ordinary life" after such an ordeal. Ironically, it was after this war—"Samuel's war"—that chemical warfare was considered too inhumane and uncivilized and therefore banned...oxymoronic as that is.

> Now we are back at the homestead. Susannah is at Samuel's grave. One Stab narrates: "She was not to blame. She was like the water that freezes in the rock and splits it apart. It was no more her fault than it is the fault of the water when the rock shatters."

[Alfred approaches her.]
Alfred: Susannah?
Susannah: Hmm? [Her thoughts are a million miles away.]
Alfred: Uh. You know how much I loved Samuel, and I think you know, uh—out of respect for him, I wanted to say it in this place...I think you know I am in love with you. [He does not wait for any response from her. He notices her face, which shows disbelief, shock, but he continues undaunted.] From the first moment I saw you, like in a novel, I uh, that's my mother's overblown romantic imagination coming out in me, I suppose.... You're not making this very easy for me, Susannah.

Susannah: Sorry. [She is stunned, trying to digest this, and to find the way to respond to him truthfully.]
Alfred: Is there any hope that you could learn to love me? No, no—not the way you loved Samuel, of course, but enough to…Susannah. We can make a life together, a happy life.
Susannah: I don't think so, Alfred.
Alfred: Sounds like you're not too sure, though. Maybe, maybe there's a chance.
Susannah: I will only cause you pain, Alfred.
Alfred: Let me be the judge of that, all right?

What a painful scene. Not on the same level as the war and the scene of Tristan with Samuel, but it is really painful to watch. The scene captures incredibly what happens when a major projection is at work as Alfred stands over his brother's grave. We know it is a projection because Susannah doesn't have a clue about Alfred's feeling for her. It comes as a total shock to her.

He—on the other hand—is absolutely convinced that she has known that he is in love with her. That is what happens when a man has such unreal fantasies about a woman. He needs to expose all these inner ideas out on the table. He needs to express this to her because it is the only way that he can test his feelings against her reality.

Alfred has been harboring all of this since she arrived. It is all a fantasy in his head, yet he has not said one word to her. His shadow knows why. His shadow knows that if he said anything, she might pop his balloon in a worse way than she popped it at this point. Susannah, on the other hand, is very connected in this scene. She is present and she is no way vague. She says, "Oh no, Alfred." She demonstrates great honesty and courage when she says "no" in the face of pitiful, pleading love, but she must if she is not to contribute to the tragedy. (All the more courage is required because it would be so easy for her to feel sorry for him.)

But Alfred does not listen to her nor stop in his persistence urged on by his now compulsive fantasy that it might work out between them. Instead, he tries again. He says, "Oh, but you don't sound sure." Whenever there is a gap, or a vacuum, a man's romantic anima will rush in to fill it up, and the woman has to stand firmly and say, "No, I would only cause you pain." Susannah says that very clearly to him. She has great integrity here.

But Alfred never quits. He never lets it go. He lets his pain and his jealousy and his resentment grow. Then he writes to his mother—the most unrelated mother on the planet—and thanks her for her understanding. He writes to her during the falling out with his father, which is soon to follow. It is painfully clear that he doesn't understand the situation, but he keeps it going, never giving up. Alfred is the unredeemed one; the one who will not stop and put an end to his own disappointment, his own hurt feelings. Most of all, he will not put an end to his own power drive that remains unconscious to him. It is Alfred's Fall.

In the midst of all this pain and suffering, we have the transformation of the warrior and his return. Tristan finally returns home, having lost the madness of the war. It is One Stab who sees him riding home from afar. He then tells Decker, who cries out to the Colonel: "Look!" Everyone in the household celebrates his homecoming, including the reluctant Alfred. But later at Samuel's grave, Tristan faces his guilt in a terrible, wrenching scene:

Tristan: [In deep sorrow, he is sitting at the grave. Susannah approaches.] Oh, God, I couldn't save him.
Susannah: Of course you couldn't.
Tristan: I couldn't save him. [She embraces him.]
Susannah: It's all right.

The hero in all of us needs to experience the place where we know we can't save someone else. All of us have to come to that place, over and over again. We will want to push the feeling away, and say, "Leave me in my darkness, my despair." But Susannah doesn't leave him there. "My lady" becomes the savior of the knight simply by holding him and saying "It's all right." That is enough. It doesn't allow a man to stay in his feeling darkness. In life or in relationships, the greatest gift of a woman's love could be that simple gesture.

However, One Stab tells us that the bear's voice had not yet grown silent in Tristan. We recall that the bear is Tristan's symbolic alchemic animal. It began with One Stab wrapping him in a bearskin when he was born, and teaching him the ways of the hunt. Next came his initiation into physical danger, his encounter with the bear, in which he cut off the bear's claw and wore it around his neck. Throughout the story, One Stab constantly tells us where Tristan is, in relationship to his bear. Examples: when the bear has overcome Tristan, or when he hears the bear's voice inside him, or when the bear has grown silent. There is a constant reference to Tristan and the bear, and we may notice that there are different stages of the bear throughout the film. At the end of the movie, Tristan dies in an encounter with the bear, and One Stab tells us "it was a good death."

When we talk about the bear, what then are we talking about? The bear is the great alchemist here for Tristan. He is the one who "stirs" Tristan's energies—the fires of libido, of psychic energy. The wildness of Tristan's energy was at times too great for this ego to contain and the wildness broke him. He had to retreat. He had to go away and then, he had to return. Surprisingly the "bear's voice could again be heard in him," and once more, he had to go away to tend to the bear inside him.

We all have those places where life becomes too much for us. This is not just about a western movie. This story is about our broken places as well. Ernest Hemingway wrote, "Real strength is about being strong in the broken places." That is the paradox. If you go down into the broken places, into the brokenness, into the blackness of alchemy, transformation emerges.

Tristan has returned home, but it soon becomes apparent that the bear's voice is still inside him. Meanwhile, Susannah is in love with him, and they have finally gotten together. [They are bathing together in a warm spring in nature.]

> Susannah: Tristan, if we have a boy, I'd like to call him Samuel. If it is a girl, Isabel. I so love you. And you'll tolerate me because of how much I love you. Tristan?

[Tristan is not present. His eyes are far away, staring.]
> Tristan: Hmm? [Finally aware of Susannah, the real woman there with him.]
> Susannah: Oh, nothing.

Now Tristan is "in the soup." He and Susannah have finally connected, driving the wedge ever deeper between Tristan and

Alfred, who has left for the city. Jung says that the anima and the animus conspire to get people into the mess of life, into the soup. There is Alfred, leaving for Helena, Montana, the growing city full of life for him. Susannah is bubbling over with excitement because she has finally connected with Tristan. But where is Tristan? He is with his bear, gripped in a mood. He is not there with her at all. He is now in a relationship with Susannah, and it is not what he thought it would be at all. Remember the anima is all of a man's fantasies about a woman and what a woman should be. Susannah has carried that for him, but now he faces a real flesh and blood woman. There is talk of marriage, and she fantasizes about children, and carrying on the family names. Gratefully, he cannot get out of the soup. This predicament is exactly what the gods want.

Later, the two of them are in the bed, sleeping. Susannah awakens and reaches over warmly to caress Tristan. She then notices his wound from a horse mishap, while Tristan, prompted presumably by a nightmare, reaches for his knife, and is ready to stab her. His agitation awakens him. Susannah recoils, startled and horrified. Now Tristan realizes he must leave and urgently tend to the bear inside himself. The violence of the knife and the nightmare here make us realize that the bear carries Tristan's violent aggression. He knows now that it makes him dangerous to others, especially to women—to the feminine.

This is the place where every man knows he must learn "to make peace" with his rage, his violence and his mean anger. It is a big work. Big as a grizzly! Unfortunately, he fails to tell Susannah (just as Samuel had failed to tell Susannah when he left for the war.)

Track 7, The Farewell

[He is packing his horse to leave.]
Susannah: Were you going to say good-bye? [No response.] Tristan? [He continues to pack.] How long will you be gone?
Tristan: Not long. A few months.
Susannah: I can make it better for you.
Tristan: No.
Susannah: If we'd had a child, or if I were pregnant, would you still be going?
Tristan: Yes.
Tristan: Don't do this.

Susannah: Just give me a chance.
Susannah: Look at me. Please, look at me. [He looks at her. He is present. His eyes fill with tears.] I'll wait for you. However long it takes. [He nods his head.] I'll wait for you forever.

[He turns away, finishes packing his horse. Susannah walks away. Susannah, the Colonel and the household then are gathered outside, watching Tristan ride away.]

Susannah: Will he come back?
Colonel: I don't know. I don't know. [One Stab speaks in the background.] Stab says yes.

[Tristan rides away. Isabel Two takes to the woods and runs after him. Then she stands at the edge of the clearing, watching.]

Susannah has risen to the occasion. She would not let him stay in his mood. "Look at me." She insists that he be present to her. It takes courage for a woman to go up to a man's mood and be more feminine than the mood, and say "I am going to break its grip on you, damn it. Look at me." But she must have seen the tears in his eyes, or been overcome by her own sentiment, because then she did something that every romantic does, and it is a sin. She said that line that people should not say because it will come back to land on their lips with fiery coals—just as it did in this story. "I'll wait for you," she said, "forever." As soon as she says the forbidden words, he is gone; the bear has him. It is Isabel Two, the little girl, who runs after him as he rides away. We know that she has already laid claim to Tristan and that she is the one who said earlier that she would marry him. Rather than Susannah, Isabel Two will be the mother of his children. Further proof of why Susannah's "romantic" statement was foolish.

But one cannot fault Susannah too much. The men over and over in the story betray her. They know nothing of her human frailty; they do not look that deep. First it was Samuel who left her for a war. Then Tristan, just when she finally had him after all that longing. Finally by Alfred, who proposed over Samuel's grave and her broken heart for Tristan.

How tragic Susannah is. She carries the weight of every woman who has been betrayed by men in love. No wonder that here and later, she is finally crushed by it all.

The Colonel stands, watching Tristan ride away, not knowing if Tristan will ever return. He does not collapse in grief, but stands, watching. Remember, the myth of *Tristan and Isolde* comes from Cornwall, as does the Colonel. It is the "old place." In England, the men are taught to have a stiff upper lip—men don't cry and they don't get crushed when hard things come. This seems to be masculine strength, but it could also be unrecognized repression. In this case, it is strength.

The Colonel stands in the face of everything. For men especially, doing the work of individuation means that they build up their ego strength so that they can stand—like the Colonel—in the face of unbearable grief, unbearable pain. But, not always.

Here comes the explosion that has been boiling behind the scenes. Alfred comes home:

Alfred: Father, I have come to ask for your blessing.
Colonel: My blessing?
Alfred: You see these gentlemen, and—
One of the men: And a great many others I might add.
Alfred:—they're urging me to run for office.
Colonel: Office? What sort of office?
Alfred: The United States Congress.
One of the men: That's how highly we think of your son in this county, Colonel.
Colonel: Well, Alfred. [He laughs. All join in the pleasure of his laughter. Then he turns and addresses the men. Directly. Soberly.]
What do you gentlemen hope to get out of this?
One of the men: I beg your pardon, Colonel?
Colonel: I've spoken plain English. What do you want for yourselves if my son is elected?
Alfred: Father, I really don't think that these gentlemen—
Colonel: [Turning to Alfred] Didn't you ask that question yourself? Or do you honestly believe these good gentlemen back you out of a sense of patriotic duty and your own inestimable worth?

Alfred: You forget yourself, Father. I am no longer a child.
One of the men: Colonel, the Congress—
Colonel: Congress is government, Sir. I worked for the government once.
Alfred: Father, the issues that we—
Colonel: Indians. Indians were the issue in those days. I can assure you gentlemen that there is nothing quite so grotesque as the meeting of a child with a bullet, or an entire village slaughtered while sleeping. That was the government's resolution of that particular issue, and I've seen nothing in its behavior since then that will persuade me that it has gained any wisdom, common sense, or humanity.
Alfred: Well, gentlemen. My father—for whom I have the deepest respect—says that the government has neither wisdom nor humanity. I will then consider it my absolute duty as my father's son to bring both wisdom and humanity to the United States Congress. I thank you for your blessing, Father. Gentlemen?

[He escorts the men out of the house, and then sees Susannah on the porch.]

Alfred: Gentlemen, would you mind waiting for me in the car?
The men: Certainly. Yes.
Alfred: Susannah, are you all right?
[Susannah is holding Tristan's letter. Tristan has written to her, saying, "All we had is dead, as I am dead. Marry another." She gives the letter to Alfred who reads it.]
Alfred: Ah. I don't know what to say. Tristan's always been wild. You love him for that.
Susannah: Do I? Yeah, I suppose I do. [She weeps.]
Alfred: He does love you. Shh…. [He comforts her.] Sort of…..

[The Colonel—having come out on the porch—calls out to Alfred, warning him away from Susannah.]
Colonel: Alfred? She's to be your brother's wife!
Alfred: Yes, though you might better remind him of that fact.
Colonel: He's not here to defend himself.
Alfred: No, he's not. But I see you are here to defend him, and

what is his, even though he has abandoned her, and you. And I won't even speak of whom else he abandoned. (His long-seething resentment over his father's "favorite" finally erupts.)
Colonel: Damn you, boy. Don't you blame my son for Samuel's death. Samuel chose to be a soldier and soldier's die. Sent to their slaughter by men and government. Parasites, like you. [He physically grabs Alfred.] Damn and blast you.
Alfred: Damn you.
Colonel: And damn you too. [Turns to Susannah.]
Alfred: Shut your mouth. You leave her out of this.
Colonel: You get out of my house and off my land.
Alfred: Why? Because I want to serve my country as you did, or is it because, like you, I love a woman who doesn't love me? [Susannah is physically hurt by his remark, crumpling to the ground.] He used her. And he deserted her, your darling Tristan. (His bear knows no limits now. It all comes out.)
Susannah: Oh, Alfred, don't. Please don't!
Alfred: I loved her. And I love her still. And he stole her from me. Hell, if you want to know the truth of it, he stole her from Samuel before the war. (He comes out with his real poison, saved for this terrible moment.)
Colonel: God help me, I'll kill you.
Alfred: [Throws the letter at the Colonel.] Here. Read your darling Tristan's letter. [He walks by Susannah on his way out. She is sitting on the floor, devastated.]
Susannah, you deserve to be happy.

One Stab: "Late that night we found the Colonel on the floor beside the cold fire. He could not move. His hair turned white overnight, and he became an old man. After that, Tristan sent no more letters. And as the years passed by, we would hear that someone had seen him on a ship going up some river no white man had gone up before. Stories came to us. Strange stories. And then for years, there was nothing. He was lost to us. That was all we knew. But every year in the moon of the falling leaves I would dream that the bear's voice inside him had grown silent, and that Tristan might come again to live in the world. But then the winter would come; and then another spring; and still he stayed away."

In this one scene—the climax of the story—we see all the dynamics of the family and what jealousy can do and what repressed anger explodes with, all at the worst possible moment. It even winds up smashing the woman Alfred says he loves.

It is interesting to note that Jung had the same view of government as the Colonel does, and the Colonel is trying to wise Alfred up when he asks the entourage, "And what, gentlemen, do you expect to get out of this?" It is also the first time that we meet the two Irishmen, part of Alfred's political group of backers, who will be behind the rest of the disasters that befall the Ludlow family. How is that for a twist of evil?

Alfred and the men are caught off guard—they all think the Colonel was laughing because he is so pleased at the prospect of his son becoming a Congressman. Instead, he set them up, ready to cut right through their manipulation and show their deviousness. Alfred comes to their defense—"But, of course not, Father," he responds in his naïve sincerity. He has not yet recognized a fundamental truth of life—that there is never anything for free—ever. We have to pay for everything we get. If we don't, then full payment will be extracted from us. Jung, in his Houston film interview says: "Everything in life costs. The greater the value, the more the cost."

We too could be fools like Alfred, and think we have allies when in fact we are being used. We could be over-trusting like Alfred and think we are doing a noble thing, when in fact we are being a tool of evil. We could be a sentimentalist like Alfred, and echo the words of George Bernhard Shaw by talking about wisdom and humanity, while putting evil into action, and then protest innocence with, "*C'est moi?*" That is the proverbial "road to hell paved with good intentions." Good intentions do not count. What counts is that you look at things with a stark, harsh clarity, which cuts through the self-deceptions, sentimentality and foolishness, and that you know your own shadow, which always wants "something for nothing."

In addition to the open conflict already raging between the Colonel and Alfred, the letter has come from Tristan, exposing all the rawness and the pain of this family, as well as Alfred's jealousy. Alfred just blurts it all out—"I love her still," and "Why do you defend this man who has abandoned her and you?" The Colonel, brilliantly and with great heart, replies, "I'll kill you if you don't get off my land."

If we were to take Alfred's side, we, like him, might ask, "Why do you defend this man?" What does Alfred do to make the Colonel react in this way? Does not Alfred have a right to say what he feels? Not if he harbors poison. Not if he blames Tristan for Samuel's death. Not if he blames Tristan for Susannah. The Colonel makes his response clear, saying, "Samuel died because he went to war, and that is what soldiers do." At this point, the Colonel can hardly contain his rage at Alfred's sniveling cowardice. As with all weak people, Alfred does not realize his own behavior provokes such response.

Alfred continues to sin against the family again and again, and this weakness is what the Colonel sees, and what he will not tolerate. Alfred cannot keep that jealous, secret poison that has been festering in his black heart, and in one stroke he slanders Tristan and Samuel and Susannah—all of them. That is what wild passion does. All of his black secrets come pouring out, even though Susannah tries to stop him, and he can never take it back. To add to the growing tragedy, Tristan's letter causes the Colonel to be stricken down, and he grows old overnight.

Track 7, Farewell

And what of Tristan? One Stab tells us that many years have gone by, and now he dreams that "the bear's voice has grown silent." After these years of hibernation, after these years of inner work, after these years of transformation, the wild, savage energy that had ripped Tristan apart has grown silent, and he might one day again enter into the world. That is a great description. When you deal with your darkness, you are able to enter the world again and become a part of it. Jung said that when you confront your shadow, when you accept it, then you are able to come back into the world again and be a part of it, and link to all humanity on a whole new level.

Track 8, Tristan's Return

That feeling is wonderfully portrayed in Tristan's return. He is transformed. He is riding home, escorted by wild horses, wearing a suit and tie and overcoat, and his clean hair flows back in the wind. What an image! One Stab first hears the sounds of the horses, the thunder of the wild horses as in stampede. He goes out to meet that sound, sensing the moment. The horses are riding with Tristan, escorting Tristan home. His outfit is very different from the wild, dirty look he had earlier. He comes back with that wonderful, free energy—but the horses ride with him, accompanying his return, and then as a herd they enter the corral, One Stab shutting the gate behind them. The horses symbolize his energy that can be corralled. It is a wonderful image of energy that can be ridden, bridled and carried when you understand the symbolism of wild horses.

Tristan must now face all the changes that have taken place since he left. That means seeing his father—crippled by a stroke—and the loss of the family fortunes, as well as Alfred's rise in politics. He learns that Susannah and Alfred are married, and live in Helena. The meetings now between the knight and his lady are especially painful to watch.

[Tristan finally goes to Helena to see Susannah. She is once again in white, and attended by a nurse—she is not thriving.]

>Susannah: Forever turned out to be too long, Tristan.
>Tristan: I know.
>Susannah: Here. [She removes a bracelet he has sent her.] I don't want it. [Notice she was wearing it though she did not expect his visit.]
>Tristan: They told me this was magic. That whoever wore it would be protected. [He gives the bracelet back to her. He turns away then to leave.]
>Susannah: Tristan? Don't you want to see Alfred?
>Tristan: It is probably better that I don't.

[Later, Tristan has married Isabel Two, and has two children. Isabel Two is accidentally killed in a confrontation with the police paid off by the Irish mafia. Tristan has been jailed for beating the policeman who shot her, and Susannah comes to see him.]

>Tristan: [Surprised by her visit] Susannah?
>Susannah: I am so sorry to hear about Isabel. We all loved her.
>Tristan: How are you?

Susannah: I never get to see you. [She tries to be cheerful.] I gave a speech the other day.
Tristan: You did?
Susannah: My first public engagement. It was, um, on the responsibilities of women, um. On the responsibilities of women in—[She falters.] It's good to see you. [Tristan begins to cry, they embrace. She kisses his face, his eyes.] Oh, my God.
Tristan: I'm sorry. I'm sorry. [He sees what pain she has carried for him.]
Susannah: I still sometimes dream that I am the mother of your children… I wanted her to die. Or maybe I even wanted Samuel to die.
Tristan: You had nothing to do with Samuel's death. You had nothing to do with Isabel's death.
Susannah: [Looks at him. Begins to wish out loud] Sometime…
Tristan: [Quietly. Firmly.] Go home. Go home to Alfred.

Even after Isabel's death, Tristan won't allow her to imagine them together again. We have talked about the background myth of *Tristan and Isolde* and it is important to notice the meaning of the name, Isolde. Isolde means "inconsolable one." That is what happens to the woman in this story. The darkness descends; Susannah becomes the inconsolable one and she kills herself. At Susannah's grave, Alfred pours out his bitterness to Tristan:

Alfred: I followed all the rules—man and God's. And you followed none of them. And they all loved you more—Samuel, Father, and even my own wife.

Track 7, Farewell

Susannah carried the betrayal of the feminine. She carried it all, for the entire family, and it finally crushed her. That is one level of meaning in her life and death. There is also her betrayal of her own heart. When she said, "Forever turned out to be too long, Tristan," she knew that she had betrayed her own heart. So much of her heart was in that vow. A woman cannot do that because the betrayal of her own heart will kill her. It is very different from the "heart" dream earlier. We are finite and we cannot say "forever." All those vows we make—we cannot say them. So many people have learned that now.

Alfred acknowledges his defeat to Tristan. "I kept all the rules, and still she loved you more." That sets up the final showdown. This is a wonderful scene, and it is important to take notice of all the people and where they stand.

[Tristan has just said good-bye to the Colonel. He knows the Irish Mafia is looking for him after his fatal fight with one of the O'Banion brothers. He comes out on the porch to see the other O'Banion showing little Samuel—Tristan's son—a gun. It is the gun Susannah had used to kill herself. We notice that Isabel One, the mother, has returned to the ranch. She is in the background, holding Isabel Three, Tristan's daughter.]

> O'Banion: Now, Samuel, this is a gentleman's gun. It is a lot smaller, but just as powerful.
> Tristan: Samuel! Samuel! Come here!
> O'Banion: Now, go along now—
> Tristan: [To Pet Decker and his mother] Get him in the house.
> O'Banion to Tristan: He's a fine boy. You know we're not here to arrest you.
> Tristan: You take me to the woods. I don't want my boy to see. Let's get on with it.

[The Colonel emerges from the house, wearing his great animal skin coat.]
> Colonel: HEY!
> Tristan: [Warns him with his tone] Father…
> One of the men: Colonel Ludlow, sir.
> Colonel: What's going on here?
> Irish man: [Mocks the Colonel, laughs] What's going on here?
> Colonel: HEYAH! [He says it in a way to incite a horse, as if digging a spur, and saying Heyah! One Stab is holding the reins of Tristan's mare. The horse rears up, and Colonel Ludlow reveals the shotgun hidden behind his coat, and fires. Gunfire erupts. An Irishman has a bead on the Colonel, and Tristan steps in front to protect his father with his own body.]

> Tristan: N-O-O-O-O!

A gun fires, and then emerging from behind the side of the building, is Alfred, holding his rifle. It is his shot that has saved Tristan, and the Colonel even as Tristan shouts his scary "N-O-O-O-O!" again, but this time there is a different ending. Their enemies lay dead. But it is that same denying "N-O-O-O-O!"

Alfred walks toward Tristan. Their eyes meet now in recognition and respect, their brotherhood restored. The Colonel watches.

The Colonel to Alfred: HEY!

He calls to Alfred. The father and Alfred are reunited. The father embraces him and begins to laugh, deeply, triumphantly, holding his eldest son with what can only be described as deep feeling.

[The three men survey the dead. Alfred and Tristan know that Tristan will be blamed.]

Tristan: Alfred. I want to ask you to watch over my children. Watch over Samuel.
Alfred: Brother, it will be an honor.

One Stab: "That night we buried the bodies and dumped the car in a deep pool in the upper Missouri. I remember when he was a boy; I thought Tristan would never live to be an old man. I was wrong about that. I was wrong about many things. It was those who loved him most who died young. He was a rock they broke themselves against however much he tried to protect them. But he had his honor and a long life, and he saw his children grow and raise their own families. Tristan died in 1963, in the moon of the popping trees. He was last seen up in the North Country where the hunting was still good. His grave is unmarked but it does not matter. He had always lived in the borderland, anyway, somewhere between this world and the other."

In the last scene, Tristan has his final encounter with the bear. We see Tristan coming together with the bear in the final encounter, or, to use the words of Jung, the final *conjunctio*.

Notice the change in Tristan and in the family as depicted in these last scenes?

Alfred has finally come through, and he is redeemed and reunited with the father. Isn't that scene wonderful? The mother has returned, holding the little girl, Isabel Three. Tristan is in the background. The bear is at peace. The energy has changed. Tristan is a different person. He faces his adversaries calmly, straightforwardly, and says, "Take me to the woods. I don't want my son to see." Now he is the father, protecting his son from "the madness."

The Colonel, true to form, confronts the situation head on, "What's going on here?" When he is mocked, he creates the diversion necessary to buy time, and blasts O'Banion away.

Tristan steps in front of the gunfire to protect his father. He has gone through the trials and the fire, again and again. He has gone through the crucible we all go through. He lived to see his children grow, and to meet the bear in the North Country, where the hunting was still good. The circle of life was complete. That is transformation. It is the goal we all look forward to—to be transformed and to touch into that circle of completion and wholeness.

This is the story of Tristan, the knight, that tells us that hope and transformation are possible for each of us if we pay attention, do our inner work, and grapple with our "bear." Those energies can be transformed into completion and wholeness one day.

5

The Confrontation with the Unconscious

 *One Stab: "Some people hear their own inner voices with great clarity and they live by what they hear. Such people become crazy or they become legends."*

Track 7, Farewell; Descent Into Madness

Thus begins this wonderful film. We have seen these lines introduce the story of Tristan as the knight, as the heroic personality, and the myth behind him, and we have seen that this story has many levels of meaning. Now it is time to turn our focus to the deeper levels of meaning in the story, and what this film may say to us about our own life's journey, our own confrontation with the unconscious.

According to Jung, we have just left the Age of Pisces—the Aion of Christ, who is symbolized by the great Fish. We have entered the Age of Aquarius, who is the great Water Bearer. The containers of the psyche in the past—the Church and the other institutions that have prevailed in our culture over the centuries—may not work anymore for some. They tend to be outworn and dogmatic, and their images no longer carry the numinous—the encounter with the other—for many people. Jung has concluded that this is the dilemma of modern man; for the truly modern man, there is no longer any container for the psyche, or soul. That means each person will have to carry the psyche individually. (Jung; *Modern Man in Search of a Soul*, ch. 3) The sign of the Water Bearer today means that each person's carrying is the task of the modern hero in the Aquarian age.

This is why Jung is so important to us. That was the way he lived his life. He took up his task. He heard his own inner voices with great clarity and lived by what he heard. He encourages each of us to do the same—not just to take his word for it. Now it is true that not very many people have agreed with Jung. Most of us are still looking for that container "out there," convinced that we will find it, somewhere—perhaps in some other culture or sub-culture, or convinced that somehow we can make the old containers work for us. Jung tells us that the only way we can succeed in doing that is to ignore the psyche. We have not yet accepted that Jung was way ahead of his time. Most people haven't caught up to him yet. It will take a long time to understand what he has said and to integrate it into our conscious awareness through our experience. This film shows us that consciousness cannot be accomplished by an intellectual exercise. The task for each of us begins when we are initiated by the bear—when we are wounded.

If Jung is right, the initiation by the bear is the initiation into the task of the Aquarian Age. Through that confrontation, we may begin to carry our own consciousness, our own individual awareness. That is the task of the heroic personality today. We must be willing to experience an encounter with the numinous and to confront the unconscious individually. We need to confront our own unconsciousness—to admit that we are in the dark, and to face our own evil. There are some sensitive, deep, neurotic, complicated people around today who are awakening to the fact that things just simply don't work the way they used to. These people are like Tristan, troubled by what they hear. They are wrestling with the psyche, with the bear. Those people are the most likely to hear what Jung is saying, to listen to their own "inner voices" with great clarity, and then live by what they hear. Living by what one hears in this sense dis-involves them; this is what Jung called individuation, the symbolic life.

How do we hear those inner voices? One way is to pay attention to our feeling. We have been talking about the feeling function, the function of value. Here is an example of what happens when the feeling function is left unconscious, and is projected.

In conversation recently with a fellow, mention was made about this work on the film, *Legends of the Fall*. He reacted with visible distrust, distancing himself as far as possible from this film—"Isn't that just a "touchy-feely" movie for the ladies?" Now Jung has warned us to watch out for any statement that is a "nothing but" statement— any statement which reduces something of value to a "nothing but," or an "isn't that just." We hear this statement far too often. It is a projection, a masculine projection onto the feminine. It is a fear of the feeling side of life. In that statement, women and the feminine are regularly, dramatically, subtly and unconsciously, put down. The feeling function is projected and perceived as weakness out of fear. The feminine is not about "touchy, feely." If anybody has run into a goddess on the warpath lately, you know that is not true. The feminine is not about mushiness or sentimentality. The feminine is about exquisite valuing, and exquisite sensitivity, and it can be just as ferocious and just as outraged as a mother bear, a grizzly. In light of this film, it should not come as a great shock to us to discover that the bear is connected to the feminine side of life. Bears are feminine symbols. If a man thinks it's not masculine to wrestle with a grizzly, then he has never been close to a live bear. It is an audacious task, which this film shows us.

The word we have used so much in our discussion, the word "berserk," comes from a German word that has its archetypal roots in the word meaning "bear." We have seen what it means—it means to "lose it," to become enraged. We have seen that it can be very intoxicating and powerful, that it can be an experience, which comes from "bear-likeness." We have noticed that not only was the bear his special animal, but Tristan regularly goes berserk. He experiences the "bear madness." He must leave, and ride away regularly—to tend to his bear madness. Likewise, when we ride off into the woods, it is because we cannot stay where we are. Under the right conditions, that ride into the woods can be called analysis or therapy. Should we find ourselves in a place experiencing the "bear madness," we know we cannot stay there. It is then time to confront the bear, the unconscious, in analysis. The bear demands our attention; it needs a "One Stab."

When you know that you need to leave what is here and experience something different—that is the bear. If you are like Tristan and you see that you have to ride off to get it just a little together so you don't kill somebody—that is the bear. If you find yourself suddenly acting like a goddess, or if the god Ares is waging war in your domicile, then that is the time to ride off—that is the bear. Riding off—just as it happens in this movie—happens regularly to all of us, if we would take the time to notice. It occurs when the "crazies" get us. It occurs when you want to go to the mall at midnight. One doesn't have to go to Montana to experience the bear. It doesn't even have to be a big Hollywood scene. The feeling that one must ride off somewhere, to "get the hell out of Dodge," means one is afflicted by the bear. So what is Tristan's quest as he rides off and leaves the homestead? He is "working out his crazies," his own psychological task. He is confronting the bear.

✣ ✣ ✣ ✣ ✣ ✣ ✣ ✣ ✣

In this modern great legend of romance and the great warrior, the confronted man is coming to terms with his madness and his darkness, as well as with the unconscious. That is also what happens in analysis. There, we learn to carry our own consciousness, our own awareness, and to work through the confrontation with the bear. What clues support this thesis? Let's go back to the movie and start at the beginning, which sets the tone for the whole story:

One Stab narrates: "One year…I am an old man, I do not remember the year, but it was the moon of the red grass when Isabel Ludlow, their mother, went away for the winter. She said the winters were too cruel for her. She said she was afraid of the bears. She was a strange woman anyway."

The original catalyst of Tristan's problems is made clear. Not only does the mother go away, leaving her young family, but also she goes away precisely because she is afraid of bears. She is afraid of that animal which happens to be Tristan's soul, his special animal. That caused the break between Tristan and his mother—he never speaks of her again.

One Stab continues: "That spring though, she did not return. And after that she did not come much to see us. Alfred wrote her many letters, but Tristan refused to speak of her. His world was here with me. Every warrior hopes a good death will find him, but Tristan couldn't wait. He went looking for his."

Here the difference between Alfred and Tristan is made clear.

[We see the young Tristan's encounter with the bear, in which he is clawed, but then, drawing his hunting knife, he strikes back, and cuts one claw from the grizzly. The bear limps away, and Tristan sits at the base of the tree, holding his wounded arm, where the bear has clawed him.]

> Colonel: Tristan? Tristan. Was it a bear?
> Tristan: Yes, sir.
> Colonel: Can you breathe?
> Tristan: Yes, sir.
> Colonel: Take your hand away. Take it away. Ah, boy, you're a stupid half-breed jackass. Did you know that?
> Tristan: Yes, sir.
> Colonel: One Stab put you up to this? You deserve to be dead, you know that? God knows how you've lived this long. You'll be all right, son.

That is Tristan's initiation expererience. Symbolically speaking, we could say that Tristan's encounter with the bear is his encounter with the other side, the unconscious and the collective unconscious. Not only does he encounter the bear and get wounded by her, he simultaneously makes an impact upon the bear as well. At this very early age he had this encounter, and we might notice that his initiation came after the separation from his mother, Isabel—the mother who had left him, and to whom he never wrote. He has nothing to do with her. That separation from his mother is very important for a young man.

Which son keeps writing to her and stays close to her? Alfred, the dutiful one, who began early in life to keep all the rules and who became filled with resentment and jealousy. Mothers are not always to blame for those things—sons should not stay too close. It is especially important for the masculine to separate from the mother. Both men and women need to understand that the masculine loses its vital energy when it is too near the mother. Tristan is the one who stands up to her, who separates from her, and does not mention her again. Because of that, he is the most vital of the three brothers.

Who becomes his mother? The ones closest to nature—One Stab and the Bear. They teach Tristan to grow into himself, to come home to himself. Nature becomes his teacher. Tristan encounters the reality of the psyche in that way, and thus Tristan becomes the symbol for all of us. We have all been battered and clawed by that bear. It might have taken us longer—perhaps we were age forty and not age thirteen. Perhaps we didn't go "looking for ours," or have our initiation so early in life, but that bear has clawed us all. The bear is the companion of Artemis, the goddess of nature, the symbol of the collective unconscious. The bear wounds us and makes us vulnerable to the unconscious. Wounding opens us to the unconscious.

The bear wounds Tristan at a very young age, which is the sign of a shaman, or a medicine man. In his great book, *Shamanism,* Mircea Eliade describes the initiation of the shaman, the healer or healing personality, in cultures the world over. It is an encounter, which comes at an early age and changes the initiate forever. Tristan's encounter is like that. He does not cower in the face of it. He does not turn into a wimp. He stands up to the bear and fights back, getting one of his claws. (Refer to Joseph Henderson's *Rites of Initiation,* Chapter 2, where he speaks of Jung's interpretations of the two bear dreams and their symbolic meaning.)

Of course, the Colonel is outraged—"You deserve to be dead, you know that." The real parents need to be outraged when their children behave dangerously. However, Tristan's "godfather" or spiritual guide is One Stab, and he is proud of Tristan. He encourages him in his stand against the bear.

Boys need godfathers like One Stab. They can't get that kind of fathering from their literal father because he is too close. He cannot see from far enough distance. The same is true for mothers. Children need good godmothers symbolizing Great Nourishing Mother—to stand in and to mediate for them. That is especially true for Tristan, because the close bond with his mother was broken at an early age. In this sense, the Bear became his mother, confronting him and forcing him to grow into an individuated personality. One Stab was able to hear the bear in Tristan and to mediate the bear interests.

This personal growth is what happens in therapy. One Stab, the Indian godfather who is close to nature, symbolizes what therapy is all about. The care of the psyche used to happen in churches and in families with a grandfather. However, it doesn't happen in either place much anymore because the old ways have fallen apart. As Jung said, we have entered the Age of Aquarius and the "old ways don't hold." (T.S. Eliot, *The Waste Land*)

In his encounter with the bear, we notice that Tristan is marked early on by the sign of the bear, with war paint, which tells us that this is not a peaceful encounter. In that same way, encountering the collective unconscious is not peaceful. It is not a parlor game or a tea party. The process is a fearsome, wounding, scratching undertaking. Any healer worth his salt has to have thorough searching and guiding qualities as well as a capacity for mothering and kindness. Those are the bear qualities, which make the encounter real, and life giving.

⚜ ⚜ ⚜ ⚜ ⚜ ⚜ ⚜ ⚜ ⚜

The next scene should touch all of us in our Jungian hearts if we happened to notice it. It is a very small segment, with only one line. One Stab has a pouch, of par fleche or leather, and he reaches into it and says:

One Stab: "I have these letters, many letters. Read them. They are from all of them—Colonel Ludlow, Isabel, Samuel—the whole family, the whole story. It is all written here."

The whole story is written. As a matter of fact, that is literally true. In the novella, the author Jim Harrison tells us that his wife discovered her grandfather's journals when cleaning up the old homestead and that he, Harrison, used them as a basis for the character of Colonel Ludlow.

That is a wonderful image of the journal. Did you know that your story needs to be written down, because it has to be written down to be real? The act of writing it down gives feeling value to the things that touch us. The journal can be the great container for your soul. It is the great place—like that wonderful leather pouch of letters in the film—to be kept and made a sacrament. It can be the story of your life, a private container, meant only for you. Containment means bringing all of them—the bear, the Colonel, Susannah (the anima), the medicine man, Alfred and jealousy all together in one place—the whole story. The fragments of your story are collected so that your psyche, your soul, can be contained in one place.

We are so uncontained in America. We have computers and e-mail that is privy to everybody. We have fax machines and cell phones—in fact we have telephones, beepers and computer access almost everywhere we go. We are inundated by communication in all forms.

The result is that everyone meets one another coming and going and nothing is contained. Nothing is held back. Nothing is sacred. Our information is all in the air, on the airwaves, on cable, on the net, or in the wireless world in which we live, and it makes for noise, craziness and chaos. For that reason, the silence and aloneness of the journal can be so important. Containment has a way of uniting and putting details down and making them solid, so that you can then touch them. The result is real substance, and you can "touch" your feelings. You can "touch" your values. You can know what your experience is and you will then have a record of your soul. Such is the immense value of a journal.

Letters also have an important place in the work of our soul. Reading a recent letter written by a daughter to her mother, showed the wonderful healing effect the letter had on their relationship. In a time of fireworks between people, letters can have that kind of healing effect, which talking—and especially e-mailing—cannot do. That is because it really helps to put things down in writing, to take the time to convey our real feeling, when everything is flying around and the sparks are flying, and consequences seem pretty awful. Writing in our journal or writing a letter puts the real feeling down. The English poet, Thomas Gray wrote:

> Full many a gem of purest ray serene,
>   The dark unfathomed caves of ocean bear;
> Full many a flow'r is born to blush unseen,
>   And waste its sweetness on the desert air.
>   "*Elegy in a Country Churchyard*"
>   (Lines 53-56)

If something is not written down, it seems to not bloom at all. It is unseen—as in a desert. When we write in our journals, the flower is noticed and we can touch it. The flower is not lost. We are not lost. The flower of journal writing is often mistakenly called a narcissus. A narcissus (also called a jonquil or a daffodil) is a harbinger or an early flower of spring. There is a myth behind the narcissus, and perhaps you know it. The Greek youth, Narcissus, went to the pond, and seeing his own reflection, fell in love with it, and got stuck there. That is where we get our English word, narcissism. When we are writing in our journals, and when we are relating to other people, it is helpful to remember that Eros is about relatedness. Narcissus has a problem. He can only think about himself. When you get into this work, and you face your shadow and the unconscious—your own personal unconscious—you have to do a lot of self-reflection. If you are not careful, you might get caught up in Narcissus, and get stuck there. You might turn into a jonquil. For example, when people will talk to you, and ask you how you are doing, you tell them about yourself instead of relating back to them. Or the shoe might be on the other foot—when you are talking with someone, and you ask him or her their response to something, they don't respond. They only tell you about themselves. That is the Narcissus myth at work; that is narcissism. Narcissus is a harbinger of spring and very often in any sort of renewal movement, people get narcissistic. But hopefully, like the flower, it is only temporary. It too will pass.

Recently, someone was offered a flower of generosity, by paying the other person a sincere compliment. But the response was the narcissus—the giver got to hear all about what a bad day the friend had, how hard his task was, so the compliment just went right out the window and wasn't heard at all. We all know people like that and we all have a little jonquil growing in our yard. We should try to connect it into the other side, into life—life is about relating. Life is about being in the game and about hitting the ball back to the other person. It is about responding, even when the response isn't very lovely. When you do this work of self-reflection and writing in your journal—keep the myth of Narcissus in mind in order to stay connected to life and to the people around you.

This scene of One Stab with the pouch of letters would make a great painting. It is a wonderful visualization of the power of the journal, the power of writing things down, as a symbol of that. Jung gives immense importance to writing things down. The unconscious is just that—it is not "conscious." That means it is unseen, unnoticed, and in the air, and it is the task of the human person to give it form. The first and most primary way to give it form is to write it down. It is our task to:
1. write down our reactions
2. write down our dreams
3. write down our interactions with our dreams.

That is what it means to keep a journal. There is a great deal of resistance to doing that work. The ego is lazy. We make up excuses like, "I'm not a writer." "I prefer to dance." "I prefer to visualize." "I like to paint." But Jung said that it wouldn't work that way. He said that first we need to write it down. Then we can carry out our other experiences—whatever else we might want to do. But write it down first, so that it has form.

It was also a personal, cardinal law of Jung's to respond personally to everyone who wrote to him. Letter writing has become an old-fashioned art, especially with that newcomer on the block, e-mail. E-mail is not the same as letter writing, even though we all use it, and it has become a great convenience. However, it is often impersonal. It is written in haste and lacks feeling. It is very important to respond to people on a feeling level. That is the nature of Eros, of relatedness. If Jung—the great man—found the time to respond to everyone who wrote to him, then so should we. It is a Jungian anachronism. Someone said to me recently, "You Jungians are the only people I know who still write letters of thank you and notes to people."

The answer was that letter writing and note writing is a wonderfully related thing to do. It is the connecting feeling function that is honored when you take the time and make the effort to respond. It is that tiny little feeling duty that is so important. Jung told the story of a woman who brought him some wonderful strawberries, and she had told him that she had almost talked herself out of it, thinking "Oh, no. Don't do that. Don't bother. It's really not necessary." Jung said that it can be a tiny matter, but it is important to follow that feeling duty. He called it that inconsiderable, tiny, miniscule feeling duty. (CG Jung, *Visions Seminars*, p. 5)

Picture life on the freeway, and you can see how much life those tiny feeling duties have today. Can you visualize what is happening to them out there on the highway? They have no place and they are getting massacred by the zillions. So, honoring them means standing against the tide. That action takes time, but it honors the personal side of life, the importance of the individual, and our respect for them. We find that people are surprised when we return a phone call, much less get a personal note or a letter from us. That seems positively antediluvian in the modern world. Why do we persist? Jung said that when the feeling function is lost, the Self hardens. That is the great danger of the modern psyche. The Self hardens all around us and that means that life grows hard. That means everything becomes hard, harsh and impersonal. Rather than becoming great crusaders, we can take our small stand against it by honoring our little feeling duties, the feeling function. We write a thank you note to someone who has meant something to us, or take him or her some strawberries. In this light, perhaps we can see why this very small scene of One Stab's pouch of letters carries so much value.

※ ※ ※ ※ ※ ※ ※ ※

In the next scene, there is even more about the letters. This scene reveals a great secret. We have talked about the Mother's absence and the Colonel having to be both mother and father in the family. Faced with the task of Eros, he writes:

April 13, 1913
Dear Isabel,
I'm not fool enough to try to reorder a life already lived. But I fear I have not done well raising our sons alone in this wild place. What did I know of children? I was trained to lead men. This is infinitely harder.

Isabel responds:
Dear William,
You take too much responsibility on yourself, as always. Our sons are finding their own paths. They are willful, certainly, but then who are you and I to complain of willfulness? As for Samuel, I have big news. At a Harvard tea for Amy Lowell, he met and instantly loved Miss Susannah Fincannon. And William, I know it will surprise you greatly, but they are engaged. He will bring her to Montana this summer to introduce her to his brothers and to you. So, William, please behave yourself and be as charming as only you can be.

We have discussed this scene in the development of the story, but here is another commentary about this exchange of letters between the Colonel and his wife. Symbolically, this is a wonderful example of a man writing to his anima. The secret of the Colonel's Eros, his relatedness, is that he stays in touch with the feminine side. Metaphorically, we could say that Isabel the anima is far away, over in Boston, while he is on the ranch, but his letters are his connection to the feeling side, the other. Her wonderful response at the end, "So, William, I know you will be your charming self,"—meaning of course, "Don't be a Bear"—softens him. She softens and connects him. The secret of the Colonel is that he stays in touch with the feminine through his writing. And, in that sense, Isabel is not far from him and his *inner* Isabel.

We can take that internally, not literally. The Colonel is staying in touch with the feminine side of himself through his writing, his letters—through his journal. Jung says that the way a man can stay in touch with his anima, is to write letters to her every day in his journal. The same is true for a woman with her animus. She can write to her Brad, or her Tristan, her Alfred, or her idealistic Samuel. The point is to write and to stay in touch with the other side.

For example, if a woman writes to her naïve Samuel, what might that mean? Could it mean that she would stay in touch with the young idealist in her, her naïve animus who tends to carry her away with his youthful enthusiasm? Could it mean that she gets inflated? Does a woman need to stay in touch with him? It is pretty helpful to see that she neglects to do so at her own peril. She refuses only if she is willing to re-enact the myth of Joan of Arc and get burned at the stake of her own inflation—to suffer the same fate as Samuel, in other words.

To stay in touch with the other side through writing in our journals can be life-saving, healing and redemptive inner work for our psyches. Here in the film, the connection with his anima through his letters softens the Colonel and connects him, which prepares him for the next scene, the meeting of Susannah.

[The Colonel, One Stab, and Alfred meet Samuel and Susannah at the train.]
Samuel: Oh, father, this is my fiancée, Susannah.
Susannah: Hello.
Colonel: Miss Fincannon.
Susannah: I am pleased to meet you. [She kisses his cheek.]
Colonel: [Surprised by her warmth] Oh. It's an honor.
Samuel: And this is Alfred.
Susannah: How do you do?
Porter: Here's your dog, Miss.
Susannah: Thank you.
Alfred: [In background: dog? Looks like a horse.] That's a

strange looking animal.
Susannah: This is Finn. He's a champion, aren't you Finn?
Alfred: You like exotic dogs then, Miss Fincannon.
Susannah: Very much, Mr. Ludlow. Please, call me Susannah.
Alfred: All right.
Samuel: And he's just plain old Alfred.
Alfred: You shut up.
Samuel: Where's Tristan?
Alfred: Ah, he's off somewhere. You know Tristan.
Colonel: Well, he'll be here tonight to welcome his brother home or I'll know the reason why. Well, Miss Fincannon. Please. [Offers her his arm to escort her to the car.] Did you have a good journey?

The letter from Isabel resumes:
She is such a lovely creature, William. But I feel the loss of her parents has given her a certain fragility, and at times, I think she feels very alone in the world. But she has found a new family now, hasn't she?

As we have already discussed, Susannah is the perfectly played anima woman in the film. She is the example of what Jung called the anima woman because she is so ethereal and so beautiful, so lovely and without blemish or scar, so pleasing. There is only one line in Isabel's letter about her fragility, this one line in which we are given the hint from the beginning that things will go badly for Susannah.

The film does not follow the book in its introduction of Susannah. In the book, she is immediately depersonalized and she is introduced as a manic-depressive. Gratefully, the film does not do this to her character. It is Isabel who plants the seed of warning by telling us of her "fragility," her feeling of being "alone in the world." An anima woman is pleasing because she does not have herself. She does not know who she is, and thus betrays her own values. In this film, Julia Ormond does a magnificent job of portraying such a woman. She captures the ethereal quality, the embarrassment and the pain. She embodies the anima, the idealized, projected woman within a man's soul. She carries the anima for all of the men in the family. Interestingly, it is my experience that some viewers "hated" her for this. An anima problem, indeed.

As a point of contrast, Susannah meets Isabel Two:

> Susannah: Hello. You must be Isabel Two. I have already met your mother and your father. [The ranch hand, Decker, is her father, and Pet, the Indian woman, is her mother.] How old are you?
> Isabel Two: Thirteen.
> Susannah: Thirteen. When I was thirteen I was sent away to boarding school. May I help you? [Isabel Two is helping with the chores, picking the beans in the garden—quite a contrast with boarding school.]
> Isabel Two: You are going to marry Samuel.
> Susannah: That is right, I am.
> Isabel Two: I am going to marry Tristan.
> Susannah: Then we will be sisters.

This girl, at only thirteen, knows something. She isn't ethereal. She is down to earth and she is sharp. The psyche (the soul) is sharp like that. Isabel Two reminds us that we can know such things. We can know deep within ourselves such a truth. There are many people who have known their fate even from an early age. Jung remarked that the first time he saw Emma he knew he would marry her. The skeptic in us might dismiss such things, and say "Oh, Isabel Two is just being silly, a young girl with a romantic dream." We have to respond to the rationalist—"But it happened, didn't it?" She did not say "I hope" or "I wish." She said it as a statement of fact, and it happened. When a person makes such dramatic statements of fact, it immediately makes them non-ethereal. It makes them very real.

The men do not notice Isabel Two or even the fact that Susannah and Isabel Two had this conversation and formed a bond, in which Susannah said plainly, "Then we will be sisters." In fact, Tristan still thinks of Isabel Two as a little girl after years and years have gone by. What are the men noticing and talking about? Well, they are talking about Susannah, whose beauty has caused quite a sensation. The Colonel writes his wife of the "intoxication" of "having a cultured woman in the house again." He tells Alfred to quit mooning over Miss Fincannon and come into the house. Then between Samuel and Tristan, the anima woman is again the topic of conversation, and she has Samuel spinning.

✳︎ ✳︎ ✳︎ ✳︎ ✳︎ ✳︎ ✳︎ ✳︎ ✳︎

There is another archetype at work, or more to the point, at play. The other archetype, besides the seductive anima, behind the scenes in this conversation is the *Trickster:*

Samuel: She's got me spinning.
Tristan: I bet.
Samuel: She's got these ideas and theories, and she's, she's—
Tristan: What? She's what? [He won't let Samuel change the subject.]
Samuel: Oh, nothing. So, Tristan—how did you break the mare?
Tristan: Ah, no, no. [Again he won't let Samuel change the subject.] She's what?
Samuel: Well she's sort of passionate.
Tristan: Is she a virgin?
Samuel: Good Lord, Tristan.
Tristan: You brought it up.
Samuel: Well, of course she is.
Tristan: Are you?
Samuel: Well, uh. Yes, I am.
Tristan: Can't wait until you get married?
Samuel: See, she says—Susannah thinks—we don't have to—
Tristan: Duh. [And that means?]
Samuel: No, we're not going to wait.
Tristan: And you're afraid you won't meet her expectations.
Samuel: Well, I guess I am—sort of. Should I be?
Tristan: Samuel, God bless you. You are good at everything you try to do. I am sure it will be the same with fucking.
Samuel: Tristan, really. We're talking about my future wife.
Tristan: Oh. You're not going to fuck her?
Samuel: No.
Tristan: Nope?
Samuel: No. I am going to be with her. I am going to be with her.
Tristan: I recommend fucking.
Samuel: You're impossible.
Tristan: You brought it up.

That is the Trickster. The Trickster loves coarseness, and getting right down to brass tacks, which is what Tristan does in this conversation with Samuel. The "f" word was not popular in 1915, when this story was supposed to be taking place, but it is popular today, so it is used in the film, somewhat artificially. The Trickster loves to turn everything upside down—to turn people upside down, to get people to slip on banana peels—and the Trickster especially uses coarseness. Typically, Samuel is offended. His idealistic side refuses to accept coarseness. Native Americans have clowns at their religious ceremonies to perform trickster dances at the holiest part of the ceremony. These clowns usually have their sexual appendages exaggerated—huge penises and huge behinds—and dance at the most solemn point in the ritual to keep things in perspective.

Here is a dream of a Trickster demon. It is the dream of a young client who was leaving the priesthood:
His friend, a Jungian analyst, went with him to the post office. The two postal clerks were ex-priests, Trappist monks. From there, they went to a back room and there was a huge painting of a Koshare Hopi Kachina. The painting mesmerized the young man.

The interpretation was that as an ex-priest, he was not to find his identity as a clerk to others, but rather to bring to life the Koshare Medicine Man within him. This interpretation struck a huge chord within the dreamer.

The Koshare Kachina is a clown figure for the Hopi—and in religious ceremonies—he is painted black and white. Black and white are obviously colors of the opposites. The Koshare clown is one who makes people laugh and see the humor in life, specifically in spiritual situations and dimensions. He is one who can point out the shadow opposites that cause things to happen the way they do, the opposites operating behind the scenes and behind appearances. So, too, this young man was to find his identity as an Indian medicine man, a Koshare. It is not the most esteemed position in the world, but certainly one which can put things into a wonderful perspective.

In the film, Tristan is filled with this Trickster quality. The Trickster motif is apparent in various places, winding its way throughout the story, which has something important to say to us about the ways of the unconscious. If we connect with the unconscious, we will discover that it too is filled with trickster ways. It will trick you into going into places and into situations where you normally wouldn't want to go on a bet. It will trick you out of things you want to keep, and out of places where you want to stay. Above all, the Trickster is known for his humor. The main arrow in his quiver is humor. So when we have our sense of humor, we know that we are in touch with ourselves and the gods who make everything flow. Conversely, when we lose our sense of humor, we can be very sure we have lost touch with the Trickster— not only with our Brad, our Tristan, but with the Self as well.

⁕ ⁕ ⁕ ⁕ ⁕ ⁕ ⁕ ⁕ ⁕

We return to the central myth behind this film, the myth of *Tristan and Isolde*. We first meet that myth in the kitchen of the Colonel's house, after the boys have left for the war. The house feels empty. The Colonel and Susannah are left behind. Susannah is devastated, and so rather than continue to eat in moribund silence in the formal dining room, the Colonel suggests that they join the others in the kitchen. One Stab, Decker, Pet, and Isabel Two are in the kitchen eating their dinner:

> Colonel: C'mon. Let's join them. Bring your plate. He'll be back. May we join you? Sit down. We were feeling lonely, actually.
> Susannah: [Asking Isabel Two about her pet] What is her name, Two?
> Isabel Two: Lady.
> Susannah: Lady.
> Isabel Two: Tristan's Lady.
> Susannah: In the story, Tristan's lady is Isolde.
> Colonel: You know who Isolde was, don't you?
> Isabel Two: No.
> Colonel: Ah, Decker, your daughter's in need of an education.
> Decker: Well, she can read and write, Colonel. School might be a little awkward for her.
> Colonel: I could tutor her in history and mathematics—with your permission, Decker, and yours, Pet.
> Decker: [Turns to Pet] What do you think?
> Pet: What will she do with all this education?
> Colonel: A richer, fuller life of course.
> Pet: She's a half-breed, Colonel.

Colonel: Not in this house—she is not a half-breed.
Isabel Two: Tristan calls me a half-breed. He says I am half-gopher and half hawk. [All laugh.]
Colonel: After her chores, then.
[Raising his glass in a toast.] Here's to us all.
Decker: To you, Sir, and Miss...
Colonel: And to the boys.
All: And to the boys.

In this scene, we are introduced to the myth behind the story unfolding, and the Colonel offers Isabel Two a "little education." That might be true for a lot of us—we could all use a little education about the myths that explore the deeper realities of life. And the purpose of this education is a richer, fuller life of course. He offers a toast, a toast of a little wine, calling upon the god of wine, Dionysius—sealed with a Dionysian toast to education, to us all, and to the boys.

This myth of *Tristan and Isolde* is the curse of western civilization. We say that it is a curse because it is the great projection maker, it fosters the myth of romantic love, which promises "Happily ever after." There is no such thing. Love means working things out. When two people meet and say "Happily ever after," their life has just started. Their relationship has just begun. Love is not about sailing into the sunset.

Robert Johnson, in that wonderful book mentioned earlier, *We*, writes that the single most destructive aspect of our romantic understanding of relationships is that we expect things to be "happily ever after." That expectation permeates the background. We believe that to say, "I love you" is all that needs to be said. Little do we suspect that we have just declared war on unconsciousness, on jealousy, on lust. It is the war on all things in our relationships because the point is that we need to work the fine details out, we need to fight it through. The fight has just begun.

If we play a good game of tennis, we don't say, "Well, I won," after the first shot. We must go through the games to the end of the set, and then through the sets to the end of the match. That commitment is what love is all about. It is about going to the end with someone. It is about going all the way through it to the end of the match, warts and all. Love is not about sailing into the sunset, or into the moonlight, happily ever after. If we carry that expectation in our head, and if that is what we seek, it will destroy our relationship. It is as simple as that. People fall in love with being in love—especially men. That can be a sickness, a narcissism. Men love to talk about being in love and men love to say they are in love; men preen and "moon" all over the place. Isn't that what the Colonel says about Alfred? He calls out firmly to Alfred, "Stop mooning over Miss Fincannon and get in here!" Alfred is "mooning" about Susannah, caught in his fantasies of the feminine, rather than realizing that he has some real clarifying to do, especially with her. The woman is not the repository of loveliness, and "everything clean and pure and lovely" as Samuel writes to her from the front lines of the war, with the bombs falling all around him. Love is about working things out with a flesh and blood woman who is as ordinary as he is.

How does one work it out? We can do that through communication: fighting through our moods, inner problems, and resistances, bringing all of them to the table. Repeat—bringing everything to the table. That disclosure is what kills romantic love—the "happily ever after." Then, and only then, can love be real. We notice that all the great lovers—Tristan and Isolde, Romeo and Juliet—die. They die because those romantic feelings belong only to the gods and goddesses. Those perfect feelings don't belong to ordinary human beings.

Our task—making up, living together, working through pain, getting it together—can be just as gratifying, just as fulfilling and just as meaningful as anything else in life, but we must let go of those romantic notions and expectations in order to get to that point.

This is not a popular notion in western culture. We have all grown up with *Tristan and Isolde* permeating the background, with mushy Valentine cards and romantic songs in the top forty charts. This statement is a real downer for romance and romantics, but it must be said. You may have noticed that the film is about the bear, and about the unconscious, and the bear does not act in accordance with our notions of romantic love. The two romantic fantasy lovers—whether Samuel and Susannah, Tristan and Susannah, or Alfred and Susannah—never work out their fantasies.

Tristan writes home after the war:
March 20, 1915
Dear Father and Susannah,

I'm being discharged from the army, but I cannot come home yet. I will write to Grandfather Ludlow in Cornwall and ask him to let me join him and go to sea. As for our beloved Samuel, all I can send home is his heart. Alfred will bring it back. You know the place he should be buried—up in the box canyon where he used to draw the birds.
Your son, Tristan

The best image for romantic love is the cemetery. Romantic love has to wind up there—that is what happens to it. For Tristan, the madness of war, the madness of the bear has touched him and he cannot come home. Those of you who have read the story of Laurens van der Post remember that when he fought in World War II. When the Japanese finally released him from the POW camp, he could not go home because of the madness that touched him. Tristan goes to sea, where navigation is accomplished by following the stars. Astrologers remind us that both the Big Dipper and Little Dipper constellations are bears—Ursa Major and Ursa Minor. The bear gives him orientation through madness. Tristan knows the bear's voice inside him. He knows where to go, and where not to go, in the story. Similarly, there are times when we need to know the rhythms of our own life.

A client—a lady of course—said it best when asked about Brad Pitt, who plays Tristan in this film: "What makes him so fascinating?" She replied, "Because his face looks so troubled." Men may be surprised to hear that, but that "look" is what made the ladies project their fantasies all over Brad in this movie—he is a soul man, wrestling with his soul. That is attractive to women. A soul man knows that he must wrestle for his life and that he needs to be in touch with the rhythms of nature. He gets to know when to go away—to ride off and get in touch with himself again, in order to "lose the madness."

If you want to be a soul person, you need to wrestle with your life as well as with the rhythms of nature. It takes a long time, but you will learn the rhythms of your own psyche and your own spirit. It is important to do that, if you are feeling crazy with the madness of modern life, or with the madness of war, or simply feeling crazy. When you feel crazy, you are not presentable to the social demands of your daily life, much less those of your wife and little children. Tristan knows not to go home because he is not fit for human companionship. He has to go to sea— to the woods— to the unconscious. He has to go into self-reflection. He has to go on a journey to get things worked out and cleaned up—to be transformed. There are so many bears around. Our task is to confront our bear and to be transformed. That is the task the Aquarian Age brings to each of us. *That* is what analysis is all about.

⚜ ⚜ ⚜ ⚜ ⚜ ⚜ ⚜ ⚜

6

Reflections on Evil

Track 7, Farewell and Descent

The astrological sign of Saturn, the taskmaster, is the Bear, the teacher with the whip who gets you to do the things you really hate to do. He is the one who can very often be the image of the negative animus in a woman's life as well as the image of the negative father. So we can see that the Bear is related to the feminine as the "teacher." We have already seen that it is the bear that gives Tristan the madness. It is the bear who gets Tristan to ride off and leave Susannah dumbfounded because somehow he knows it is not right for him to be with her. It is the bear that Tristan meets again and again, and confronts again and again. He is then able to come back radiant, dressed in a suit and tie, riding with the horses with his golden hair flowing in the wind. Tristan has been transformed. One Stab tells us that the bear's voice within Tristan had been stilled, and he could live in the world again.

The bear taught Tristan, so he lived close to nature, as a hunter. He was not taught by "keeping the rules" which was Alfred's way. Alfred introduced Tristan to Susannah by saying, "You'll have to forgive my brother. Your dog has more breeding than he has." Yet it is Tristan, not Alfred, who is his father's favorite son. It is a theme repeated throughout the film, and it is Alfred who seethes with jealousy and confronts Tristan at Susannah's grave:

"I kept all the rules and you, Tristan, you followed none of them, and they loved you more."

Why is that? It is a question people often ask. Here we will talk about the Bear as teacher and about the differences between Alfred and Tristan as psychological figures, as archetypal patterns of behavior. We know that Alfred was secretly in love with Susannah, but as One Stab so wisely says of Susannah:

"She was not to blame. She was like the water that freezes in the rock and splits it apart. It was no more her fault than it is the fault of the water when the rock shatters."

It was not Susannah who split this family; she did not split the opposites. Instead, we saw that is was Alfred's jealousy of Tristan which split the family and set into motion the horrible dark evil. When a person has dark secrets that are not brought to the light of day, those secrets are poisonous. Finally, Alfred confronts Tristan with his hurt and his jealousy of him at Susannah's grave: "Why did they love you more?"

We begin with Jung's comment, "The greater the light, the greater the darkness." It is certainly not all a blessing to be a Tristan, to be the father's favorite son, to have so much charisma, and to be so attractive. Those qualities will also provoke the curse of the bear and the curse of consciousness. You also get wounded, and you need to work it out. You might also experience some madness.

Let us look at this literally. What would it be like to be an Anthony Hopkins or a Brad Pitt—either of these powerful, charismatic men? We know already from Anthony Hopkins' life that he had many literal bear moments. He struggled with alcoholism, a broken family, a broken marriage, and no recognition for years as a bit actor. We could speculate those were the years he was away with his bear. If you have ever heard him talk about acting as a profession, you know he speaks from experience, and what he says is just incredible. He certainly had the experiences that make a great actor.

What about Brad Pitt—the younger man? Can you imagine the curse of Brad's handsomeness and what it must be like to have millions of women project onto you? That may sound appealing until you remember what Jung said, "to carry a projection feels like you are carrying around a dead corpse." Do you remember what the Colonel said about being worshipped by his men? "Damn fools all of them, led to the slaughter." It is an inflation to be worshipped and to be a celebrity. It explains why many celebrities have compensatory bad moods and temper tantrums; it is not "fitting" to be worshipped when you know you are ordinary. The bear lashes out, and many actors/famous people don't do very well; they crash and burn because they are too close to the sun, and not close enough to the moon. They are too close to that intense energy and do not know how to handle it. Having the energy is one thing; knowing how to live it well is another matter on a whole different level.

Tristan is mauled "by the bear," which means he is fated to deal with that energy. He must come to terms with it. He will struggle with it, because a grizzly is so enormous that it means that Tristan, too, has enormous energy. We could make a huge leap and say "that is what thousands of women say about Brad Pitt's playing the role of Tristan." Brad became Tristan so effectively that it became a breakthrough role for him. And conversely, Brad portrayed Tristan so attractively and realistically that women all over the world fell in love with Tristan. Tristan the outcast, the different one; Tristan, the special one; Tristan the wild one, who had an animalistic side to him; Tristan the one who so magically became one with the Bear energy that the bear animated him, changed him, tortured him, and worked alchemy on him. Eventually what emerged was this incredible and immensely attractive man. Because we live in this space and time, he somehow lets us see the limits of the inner appeal.

Tristan comes riding home at last, with the herd of wild horses all in tow, and he is freshened up with his great long hair blowing in the wind. It is an indelible image of a man who has somehow emerged safely and healthily. And he has emerged attractively, even more so than before. As always, One Stab gives us the clue: "The voice of the bear has been stilled." Tristan has made peace with his bear. It is a great moment of psychological realization. He has come to terms with this terrible gigantic energy within himself. It has taken its toll. It has taken a great deal of time and cost a great deal. It involved a great deal of suffering, separation and loneliness because Tristan, like his father, had "to go away." He had to leave Susannah. He had to leave all that was dear and comfortable to him, especially, it seems, feminine comfort. In short, he had to undertake "his hero's journey." He did— "and no one knew of him, " the movie says.

It is that path of which all the great religions speak (those religions with structures or hierarchies or rules or processes.) But Tristan's was a religion in the purest sense of "a contact with the divine," with a "transcendent dimension of life." That is what Tristan undertook, and he was able to come back.

But as we see in the film, there are human consequences to this. The Colonel is *stricken*. The ranch is desolate. And most *stricken* of all, Susannah married Alfred. (All of a sudden, Isabelle Two's wisdom looms prescient. "She is going to marry Tristan," remember?)

There are always consequences for dealing with the unconscious, with the bear. And usually (always?)—the ego does not like it. The collective (our group, our family, our friends) does not like it either. A huge accommodation has to be made. The more the energy and creativity are involved, obviously, the more adjustment is required. That is no accident in this case because it is a grizzly bear and grizzlies are enormous. Psychologically and symbolically it means Tristan has an enormous inner conflict/energy he must deal with. It is his fate. Or, as Jung puts it masterfully in his great essay, *Psychology and Literature* (Vol 15, CW; pp 102, Par. 158) "A person must pay dearly for the gift of creative fire."

When we see Tristan's connection with One Stab, when we see him as his father's favorite, when we see his obvious attractiveness and his "sex appeal" (that is very important here), we identify with him, we are gratified. But we forget Jung's quote. We forget about the price. We forget about the cost of that gift.

Indeed in life, that oversight can be a good thing. We have to be "inflated" even in our estimations, or wonderment would be replaced with worry. We would be too anxious about such a gift, although interestingly, Mary in the New Testament seems to have known. Isabel Two seems to have a similar sense here, oddly enough.

But back, now, to the subject of energy. Tristan, "the wild one," thus becomes a symbol of the person who is "fated" to have such energy. Hopefully, as you the reader can see from this example, it is an energy that can kill, overwhelm, and blow apart all human considerations. It is also tremendously dangerous and must be dealt with respectfully. But how many do not have a clue about "the nuclear energy" they carry within themselves? Elvis Presley and Marilyn Monroe are great tragic examples of that.

Remember Jung's quote, "A person must pay dearly for the divine gift of creative fire."

It is not surprising to find a drawing of a great fire right at the beginning of Jung's *Red Book*—his record of his own inner journey— "a great fire," seemingly exploding from the depths. It is a symbol of what happens on the great journey within when one touches the power called the collective unconscious. Also, in that same image, there is a little fellow way in the corner, bowing low before this great force. That picture is a wonderful full image of the ego, being humbled before such power. Humility. The necessary attitude of the ego here.

One wonders with all the hype of TV and advertising moguls "pushing" movies and books and music, where there is room for humility. Hopefully, such a gracious space exists in the lonely moments of the artists in their room.

Sadly, one gets the impression that quite the contrary atmosphere is found, and instead of littleness, a certain hubris grows, demanding respect. When that happens, we know "the bear" has "won" and the individual artist will be destroyed.

There is a dear price to pay. It will cost the artist a great deal, almost quid pro quo: the more you want, the more you pay. When we see the enormous villas and mansions, the incredible lifestyles "of the rich and famous," we must know that again will be extracted an equally enormous cost. One simply does not get one without the other. It reminds me of seeing this actor on a TV talk show, which happily went a little below the surface. This actor seemed genuinely happy with his more moderate success. Not as the star, but as part of an "it" ensemble. He talked about his "recovering alcoholism" and spoke realistically about his life and career. This was someone who knew his bear. Someone who had been wounded by it, but not defeated. On the contrary, he was one who had accepted it. He was so refreshing and human.

Acting is a peculiar career. It often begins lowly—waiting tables or whatever. When the archetype is finally acknowledged, if there is not a solid ego foundation won, that person would think, tragically, that success is owed him. So goes another disaster.

Alcoholics are interesting cases. As Jung alluded to William H. (founder of AA) it is easy to confuse one alcoholic "spirits" with real spirits. But "spirit" is the key. We all need "spirit." If it is not a "Holy Spirit" we will find another one, because after all, to be truly human one *has* to have spirit. It is a woeful task to constantly be trying to create spirit, or to make one up, or to "hype" it—or now, as in Bill O'Reilly's caricature "to spin it." The task is too Herculean, and often leaves the owner bereft of any energy at all, or at least exhausted, as a bear, in search of the real spirit.

One must know about one's energies. One must know about one's gifts and talents and be able to see them as archetypal energies that run through a person. Our task is to be the best conduit for them as possible, and to give credit for these gifts from whence they come, and never, never to identify with them. (Identify here means simply to think, "I am that gift, that talent," e.g. Pete Rose or Sammy Sosa.)

A priest's life is another good example. One of the things that drove many away from the priesthood was the effect of wearing the ecclesiastical collar. What does it mean to people? To whom are his parishioners relating? Was it to the person or to the collar? Maybe it was to the Church—the institution behind the collar. Where was the person? After a while, many had enough of that confusion and had to ride away, just like Tristan. The priests, too, heard the voice of the Bear; they had to ride away. Many of us have heard that bear, albeit it wasn't about the church or religion. Maybe it was about God, or one's family, or an ex-husband. Maybe one wanted to beat the bloody hell out of an ex –business partner, or wanted to lash out at everyone who has ever created hurt. In other words, the problem here is that the enemy is out there. The enemy is always they, he, she, or it. It is never within oneself.

✣ ✣ ✣ ✣ ✣ ✣ ✣ ✣ ✣

The incomparable Marie-Louise von Franz, said, "The greatest source of evil and of things going wrong in people's lives is the failure to deal with and get over hurt feelings." (Von Franz, *The Feminine in Fairy Tales;* Chap.2, p. 27, 1st Ed.) That is a remarkable statement. Hurt feelings are the greatest source of evil in people's lives, and of things going wrong in their lives. If you hold on to that evil, or to that hurt, you cause the wrath in the universe to descend upon yourself. By holding on, one does not attract good energy or healing. One does not attract justice or a good life. Instead, one causes evil. Shocking.

There are more so-called "good people," like Alfred, who go around saying they are good people, but they actually aren't. They have not dealt with their disappointments or their hurt feelings over that person, family member or institution that differ with them. Alfred is the walking "everyman" in our story. He is not only the bad guy in the movie, he is all of us who have ever been hurt, or who have been jealous of somebody we thought was better than we—we wanted to hurt them and get even with them. That is Alfred's way. That is really why the rules didn't work for him—because he's had a black heart. You can carry your God personally wherever you go, but if you have a black heart, He will never bless you. If you hold on to hurt feelings and try to get back at the one who has hurt you, you release a great source of evil, which in turn, rebounds on you. That is a remarkable statement by von Franz. Many of us do not comprehend it or realize how important it is.

We need to get over our resentments and our hurt feelings. We need to let them go. It is no wonder that one of the first steps in any twelve-step program is the step of forgiveness where one learns to get over the hurt and let it go, no matter what others have done. Who of us has not been Alfred—the secret, jealous one? None of us can pick up the first stone to hurl at Alfred—to use Jesus' words—because Alfred is in all of us.

Alfred is every insecure one of us, who, because of our own wounded feelings, has inflicted countless wounds on others. His jealousy and insecurity ricochet—just as the bullets ricocheted off the rocks—and killed Isabel Two. Those ricocheted bullets that come from a black heart kill her. Insecurity and jealousy kill the feminine. The black heart kills the feminine. That is shown so clearly in this movie. Poor Alfred—the abused child, the neglected child, the orphaned child, the wounded child, or the oversensitive child. Poor Alfred—the hurt lover, the rejected lover, the lovers' quarrels all over the world. Where will it end? It will end in bloody, unspeakable violence and death, all in the name of love.

A friend recently asked me "Why does that happen, Richard—good people who said they loved one another wind up hating one another and fighting bloody battles—why does that happen?" This is why. They fail to get over hurt feelings. The failure to get over hurt feelings starts quarrels, intensifies divorces, sets wars in motion, and kills people. It is that simple. The Fall.

In the end, Alfred stands over his soul's coffin, that of Susannah, and says, "My way hasn't worked. I have kept all the rules, and it hasn't worked." There he stands for all of us who have come to an end of that resentment and jealousy. Alfred is the broken ego, the ego that finally understands that willpower doesn't work. The rules don't work and keeping the rules doesn't work. What works? Only being in touch with your soul works. Being in touch with the feminine works. Being vulnerable and saying, "I don't know what to do. Help me." Submission and receptiveness are what works, not keeping all the rules.

In this film we learn the universe's joke about love. Love is about surrender. Finally after Alfred let go of all the rules and his jealousy, he then was able to shoot straight and save his family. That was a wonderful love story and a wonderful scene of redemption and reconciliation.

✤ ✤ ✤ ✤ ✤ ✤ ✤ ✤ ✤

One year, the author had the extraordinary privilege of being in Jerusalem at the time when Passover, Easter, the Muslim holy year, and the Greek Orthodox Easter all occurred in the same week. That does not happen every year, and the power of all of those events in all of those traditions coinciding was immense. Unfortunately, everyone there hated one another. That violent hatred is what results from splitting the opposites. Instead of being a source of inspiration and power, and honoring the different traditions coming together in that time and place, the controversy degenerates into who is right and who belongs to our group, and who belongs to that group over there. The result is a nation living in a perpetual state of enmity and alienation. That essentially is what happens in this movie and this is essentially what is going on in many lives. It is all around us. Did you know that the calendar is essentially a chart of the stars, whether we recognize it or not, and all of the world's religions, all of the world's traditions, used the stars to mark the seasons of the soul? If you think about that, it ties the church calendar to the cycles of nature and the stars, and yes, they work together harmoniously. But no one would ever know that by the enmity and the alienation and violence all around us.

What does it take to bring all of those parts of us, all those warring opposites, into harmony? It takes the confrontation with our Bear. Let us go back and look at some scenes of Tristan and his task under the tutelage of the Bear. The first scene is of Tristan struggling to free the calf, caught in the barbed wire. Let us call this scene "Tristan's Complex."

Scene: Tristan: "Quit it. Quit it. God damn it. God damn it. Ah."
[He shoots the calf.]

It is fashionable today to call that a flashback, but in reality, it is a great visualization of the term Jung coined, the "complex." There is the calf, caught in the barbed wire fence, and we know from the movie that the struggle hearkens back to Samuel's death in the war that so traumatized Tristan. Jung's definition of a complex is an emotionally charged core which, when touched, elicits strong affects that are beyond the ego's control. For instance, when your mother complex is touched, you have a big emotional reaction. When your money complex is touched, you have a charged reaction, beyond your control. Here we see an example in the scene of the poor calf, hopelessly entangled in the barbed wire, which triggers Tristan's complex about Samuel's death and his inability to save him. He "loses it." These reactions happen to all of us whenever our complexes are touched. It is important to remember that we have many complexes. You know when one of them is touched because you have strong reactions that are out of proportion to the event. Our reactions in these cases are usually irrational, and full of emotion. So the next time you are faced with one of your complexes, think of the calf hopelessly entangled in the barbed wire, and you will have an image of it. Remember also, Tristan's frustration and anger and inability to do anything about it—it is a great image. Becoming aware of our complexes is a great challenge to consciousness. That will help a great deal.

In the next scene, Tristan and Susannah are bathing in the warm spring, and it becomes clear that he is not present to her--while she is bubbling all over with plans for their lives together, he is miles away. We called that scene "in the soup," because that is just what the gods want. They want to bring Tristan into that messy place, and to get him in the soup—to be in relationship with Susannah, this fascinating anima woman, and find that it wasn't what he thought it would be at all.

The next day, Tristan has another confrontation with the bear:
Decker: Colonel! Bear up in the canyon.—might be a grizzly.
Tristan: My grizzly?
One Stab: [Speaks in Native American to Tristan.] [Not

translated.]

[The four men then go up into the canyon and have the bear sighted in the canyon.]
Colonel: You take him, Tristan.
Tristan: Damn right I will.

[The bear presents a clear shot and growls at being cornered, but Tristan does not shoot.]
One Stab: I don't know why Tristan did not kill that damn old bear. The old ones say when a man and an animal have spilled each other's blood, they become one.

It is clear that Tristan has achieved some sort of unity, despite himself. He cannot pull the trigger despite his "damn right I will." His better side wins.

This scene also gives us an interesting take on hunting, doesn't it? The film has a lot to say about hunting and blessing, and about blessing the animal and killing it at the same time.

A wonderful friend, Jack Taylor, is an avid hunter. After he read the preview of this book on *Legends of the Fall*, he called to say he had an experience with a bear, at a young age. Here is his story:

When he was a young boy, his parents took him up to Yosemite. "I was a silly teenager, and they had those signs, 'Please don't feed the bears.' Well, I acted like a stupid teenager, and I fed one of them, and the bear promptly grabbed me. It was just like in the movie. The bear scratched the hell out of me, cut my shirt, and then wouldn't let me go. It grabbed my leg, and held me in a bear lock. At that point, all kinds of people were gathering around at the spectacle, including my parents, who were frantic. Nobody knew what to do, and only kept shouting, "Call the rangers! Call the rangers!" But what were the rangers going to do? My father went to the car and got a big axe, but then he thought better of it. The bear might be stronger than his axe, and then God knows what the bear might do then. In the meantime, the bear was slobbering up and down my leg, but he didn't bite me. Finally, my father came to his senses, and remembered the salmon eggs that we had been using to fish. He took the jar of salmon eggs from the car and rolled the jar toward the bear to distract the bear. The jar didn't roll all the way to where the bear was, and I was afraid the bear wouldn't even notice. But his good nose picked up the scent, and he went over to the jar of salmon eggs, only he dragged me along with him.

Finally, he really got into those salmon eggs, and let me go—I took off. But you know, I hunt a lot, and I am in bear country all the time, but to this day I have never been afraid of a bear."

The feeling Jack conveys in his story was very similar to the feeling in this movie scene—once a connection is made, you don't kill the connected one. You do not fear it. Symbolically it means that you don't repress it. In a dream, killing something means repressing it. Killing something is a way to get rid of it. Here, Tristan does not kill the bear. He says he is going to, but the connection has been made, and he does not shoot, despite his still ornery ego.

In the next scene, we might have wished that he had killed it, because the bear overwhelms Tristan again. The first time we saw Tristan overwhelmed was after Samuel's death in the war—that was indeed Tristan's "break." We'd probably call it a "nervous breakdown" today. In this scene, the bear makes its presence known in all of its irrational rage. Tristan, the Colonel, Decker, and One Stab have gone into the saloon for a beer.

> Colonel: I said four beers, Mr. Sexton.
> Barkeep: And I said, "No Indians."
> Colonel: He's quite civilized, I assure you.
> Barkeep: Yeah, yeah.
> Tristan: Why don't you give him a beer?
> Colonel: Stay out of it, boy.
> Tristan: My father said 'four,' didn't he?
> Colonel: He heard me. Mr. Sexton and I are just about to reach an understanding. Isn't that right, Mr. Sexton?
> Tristan: Just give him a goddamn beer.
> Colonel: Tristan, stay out of it. I said stay out of it. Damn you. Damn fool. You're just spoiling for a fight with a man that outweighs you by twenty pounds. Just now as we speak, he is searching in his bar for some kind of weapon—isn't that right,

Mr. Sexton?—to split your stupid skull and leave you stone dead, and good riddance to you. Now leave it.
Tristan: I want four beers. Now.
Barkeep: Now there's the owner and he says he doesn't want to sell you any.
Tristan: [At this point, Tristan bashes the bartender's head and holds his bleeding head down, saying:] Get back. Now you see this man. Do you? His name is One Stab. He's a decorated elder of the Cree nation, and he has counted one hundred coups of his enemies. He's a friend. He's thirsty.

One Stab narrates:"I think it was the bear's voice he heard deep inside him."

Here is a visualization of going "berserk." It happens when the bear has you, instead of you having the bear. It is not being in conscious relationship with your anger. This is the scene that many civilized folk are afraid of. It's too bad—in a way—that we don't have more of Tristan in us. After we bash a few people, we get afraid of our anger. Or even worse, a lot of people even have it in reverse. A lot of us have never bashed anyone in our lives yet, and have gotten afraid of it by hearsay.

Maybe we need to bash someone. We need to experience that rage. Von Franz describes this in a beautiful section in *The Feminine in Fairy Tales*. So does Eliade, in *Myths of Initiation*. To experience this rage is to experience the total justification of honest-to-god justified anger. It makes you feel inflated, and at one with the gods. That is Tristan here. The poor bartender witnesses it at a terrible price. The Colonel tries to say, "Stay out of it, you stupid fool." But the bartender pays the price of an angry and righteous Tristan. I am sure that most of us have been there. We may not have bashed someone's skull in, but certainly we have let someone experience our wrath, someone who didn't deserve it. Did you notice the Colonel's face? The father's look is very telling; it is one of horror.

Now let's listen again to what One Stab says as he describes that scene: *"I think it was the bear's voice he heard deep inside him—growling low, in dark, secret places."*

It is a great scenario of how our anger drives us to past, dark, secret places (to quote One Stab.) It is One Stab's description of going berserk, of being run by your complex. This says a lot about the dark side of anger and explains why many of us are afraid of it. There is no other emotion that causes people so much trouble as anger. But anger like a grizzly is also of great use in overcoming obstacles, so it shouldn't be given a bad name. It is especially important when overcoming the obstacles of injustice, which is what the bartender represents here.

The problem, then, is how to express anger. Tristan gives us an example of how not to express it, but don't forget the context—his anger is about to lead to his riding off, because he knows he needs to get the bear in shape inside himself. He cannot remain like this because he is not humanly social at this point.

The opposite of Tristan is those of us who cannot even get in touch with our Grizzly—we have to ask, "where's my grizzly?" Do I ever feel it immediately, like Tristan did in the bar? That would be to touch one's instinct, to allow one's instinct to live, to have a life. Some of us don't allow it to live. Those are the two opposites.

Therapeutically, healthy anger is very important, and many times, one over-reacts. One overshoots the mark at first, because one is out of habit with this instinct. You wake up to your anger in therapy or in analysis, and you discover tons of it. It weighs as much as a Grizzly. Not surprisingly, it may come out inappropriately on the bartender, or on family members. Fortunately, we can have a way of dealing with that even if it means to say, "I'm sorry," or "I was out of sorts," or "I was out of control." But, if one sticks with it, and continues on this way, it can become more of a balancing act. One learns to express one's anger in a more human way, not so enraged like a grizzly bear but rather just as an angry person. We would express it more in a more related, more appropriate way—not blasting the other person away, but communicating in a way that the other person can take it and understand that we are angry. Expressing anger takes a lot of work and a lot of ego strength to be able to convey in this way. Jung gives two bear dreams as initiatory experiences in *Essays in a Science of Mythology,* pp 229-245.

Jack Sanford has a masterful section on the different kinds of anger in his wonderful little book, *King Saul.* Learning to express anger in a related way is very important so that is where the journal and those letters come in very handy. It is very important, to be able to contain your grizzly in your journal, where it can help to mediate the bear, the grizzly. "To mediate" means to soften, to balance, touch up, make presentable. In other words, it means to humanize one's anger.

To use Jungian jargon, it means to get the shadows or the negative animus or the negative anima out of the way—those inner creatures in each one of us who often come across as aroused grizzlies and mess up the whole scene. They are the ones who will instinctively try to get back at the one who has hurt you, before you even have a chance to think. And they will try to do it violently, the way Tristan does to the bartender. Most people cannot handle that kind of anger, and rightly so.

This is why journal work is so important. To contain the grizzly means that the shadow, or the negative animus and the negative anima are not popping off at the person who has disappointed you, or let you down. It is so important to get these inner characters out of the way. They cause the black heart we have talked so much about—that resentment and jealousy and failure to get over hurt feelings. Once they get into the act, everything they do is pure evil.

Remember this important fact: When the negative anima or the negative animus is speaking, everything they say is pure evil. What they declare is never helpful, never redemptive, and never enlightening. Despite all the "pros" you hear in your head—all the professional, expert, or holy voices you use to back you up—the negative animus and the negative anima are never redemptive. In the book on the film *American Beauty*, we discuss this in great detail. If you can get back to the origin of the hurt, and work it out with the other person, then you have restored the human, related quality. That is where the animus possession or anima possession will walk out, because that is where it first walked in—at the place where you were hurt. I remind you again of that striking quote from von Franz: "the source of things going wrong in people's lives is the failure to deal with and get over hurt feelings." She says that about women, specifically, but here we include men as well. Both men and women have to learn about the grizzly, the one who goes berserk. It is exceedingly important in the everyday life of all.

The next two scenes of Tristan illustrate the point dramatically for us:

Scene One: Tristan—in the grip of a dream or a mood—awakens, grabs his hunting knife and almost attacks Susannah, who is in the bed next to him.

Here is a dramatic example of possession. It is a great image of the power of a nightmare, of what the negative anima in a man or the negative animus in a woman makes you want to do—literally. It makes you want to kill the other person. We must recognize that fact and gloss over it. We must recognize that fact and ride off—as Tristan has the grace to do in the film. It was a redemptive act for him to ride away. It means one should have the smarts to recognize when one needs help, when one can't contain the bear anymore. We want to redeem riding away, and we call that analysis. Riding away means having the smarts and the humility to ask for help and making sure you get it. The knowledge that one needs help is a great redemptive act.

Tristan leaves Susannah and rides away. He has been shocked awake, awakened to the danger in himself. She has the sweetness to say, "Can't I make it better for you?" but that is the lament of every woman who has not faced the fact that she can't. She can't make it better for him. It is his problem, the man's damn problem. You cannot make the man better. He's got to make himself better. That works both ways. None of us can make another person better. Each has to do it himself.

In the next scene, he is totally possessed by the bear, and it leads to a terrible conclusion.

Tristan is traveling the world in his possessed state. He writes to Susannah.

Dear Susannah,

I have become a hunter. Tell Stab there are creatures here that cannot even be found in books. And I have killed them all...Susannah, all we had is dead. As I am dead. Marry another.

As we watch Tristan travel the world, we see the results of his possession. At this point in the film, there is a ghastly scene of Tristan in a brothel. So much for the glamour of the current obsession with pornography. It is not glamorous at all. That is a telling scene in the brothel. It takes the glamour away from disconnected sex. He has become a hunter, identified with killing. He writes to Susannah, telling his anima how disconnected he has become from her. Unfortunately at this point he seems to have no regrets about that. He seems almost proud of it. To complete the picture, there is the brothel, and the drugs, and the scene on the ship where he is being held in restraints as he screams deliriously.

In Jungian terms, this is the moment of Tristan's death, a psychological moment of death. Tristan declares it so: "All we had is dead as I am dead." That is the absolute darkness of the mother complex. When a man gets so possessed that he is totally without hope, and all is lost, he is willing to give up everything that is dear to him. When he projects this upon Susannah, he is in the absolute darkness of his mother complex. "Marry another. I am dead." In the myth, that is the complete desolation of Isolde. It is the nadir, the bottom, the lowest point of Tristan. "I am dead to myself. I am not myself anymore." But hopefully it isn't the end for Tristan. Jung says, "Just as nature reaches her lowest point, she reverses herself." That is why one should never give up on anyone. A complete renewal is possible out of the darkest places.

✣ ✣ ✣ ✣ ✣ ✣ ✣ ✣ ✣

One Stab narrates: "As the years passed by, we would hear that someone had seen him on a ship, going up some river no white man had gone up before. Stories came to us—strange stories. And then for years, there was nothing. He was lost to us. That is all we knew." [The scene is of the homestead, looking desolate, unkempt--the visual image of depression.]

This is the wonderfully, terrible image of what happens when the ego is overwhelmed by the unconscious in depression. It is a visualization of being overwhelmed by the unconscious. The leaves accumulate around the homestead, and things go to pot. There is no life in the place. It is decrepit. It is a visualization of the ego that has abandoned the Self, or is abandoning the Self. We no longer care or tend to the daily stuff. "He was lost to us." The hero is lost to them. We lose hope and we give up. Things turn bleak and we feel hopeless. One Stab says this masterfully here.

One Stab continues: "Every year in the moon of the falling leaves, I would dream that the bear's voice inside him had grown silent, and that Tristan might again come to live in the world."

The dream does not allow One Stab to give up on Tristan. Here is One Stab's understanding, his wisdom to listen. Where does it come from? It comes from a dream. He says that every year at a certain time he would dream that the bear's voice had grown silent in him. Dreams come from a deeper place and dreams come when we need them to come. Dreams come when the ego doesn't have strength to hope anymore. Dreams come when the fragility of our own existence gets too much for us. Dreams come to give us hope when life seems hopeless.

Recently, someone blurted out this dream to me—he said that in the dream a tornado was coming, and it was really scary. He was running around the house to get the children, and then he brought them down into the basement to make sure they were safe. He then went out and got all his friends and neighbors and brought them into the basement as well. "The tornado was coming and we were all getting ready for it," he said. Now I happened to know that he was worried about an impending outer crisis in his life when he told me the dream and so I said to him, "You know what the wonderful thing is about your dream? You have a basement. You have a basement in your psyche." He had not even noticed that in his frantic state. That is a perfect image of the ego. The ego does not notice the healing thing. It gets so worried and so caught up in the world. It gets so caught up with the obvious, that it misses that there is a basement for protection. The hero will come back. Therefore, the next time you get frantic, ask for a dream. One Stab has a dream for all of us to remember. This memorable moment shows us the helpful and healing power of dreams.

The central drama in the movie is Tristan working out his salvation through the Bear. That is why the end of the film is so beautiful and wonderful, not terrible. One Stab calls it a "Good Death." We need to keep in mind that this is the hero's journey of salvation—working out salvation through having it out with your own bear, as you need to do. That means having it out with your instincts; having it out with your resentments and jealousy; having it out with your wildness and your craziness. That sets the stage for the next scene, which is the promise of One Stab's dream—Tristan's return. It is the culmination of Tristan's journey: remember it took three times of riding away for the transformation to be accomplished. Tristan's return is the fulfillment of the dream's promise, and it is the best scene in the whole movie, which is filled with great scenes.

Track 8,
The Return

As we watch the return, listen to the music that accompanies it and captures it wonderfully. It is quite a transformation. Tristan is finally back. The hero has returned and is available for the ego. The ego has been healed. Analysis is working, so we can return to our real lives again. Notice that it takes an exceedingly long time. Notice also that it happens when things look darkest on the old homestead. Jung says that if you will go all the way down with something, nature will reverse herself. Just at the time you feel really hopeless, when "they're really going to get you this time," just when "the banker is really after you," or "the divorce court is after you," or "the kids are doing you in." Whatever the big fear is, or the outer danger you face—Jung says that if you will really stick with it and go all the way down with it, you will have this kind of reversal. But it is imperative to go with it and to pursue it to the depths. Then you receive a similar homecoming. This is a beautiful scene.

> Later, Tristan meets Isabel Two. He meets the real woman. [Tristan is in the barn, and playing with a puppy, one of a litter belonging to Isabel Two's dog, Lady Isolde.]
> Isabel: He likes you. Welcome home.
> Tristan: [Looks up, sees her, how grown up she has become.] Isabel?
> Isabel: I want you to have him.
> Tristan: I have something for you too. I brought I back. It's from Ierapetra. That's in—
> Isabel: Crete.
> Tristan: Crete. Yes.
> Isabel: I know where it is. Your father taught me European history. [She takes the small ring, meant for a girl. Puts it on her fingertip and shows him] A little girl—that's me, right? Welcome

home, Tristan.

The little girl has grown up, and she insists that Tristan take notice. This is a wonderful moment. It is also a wonderful advertisement for education. Remember, the Colonel had said that she needed to be educated enough, to be broadened enough to enrich her life. On an inner level, the anima and animus need to be educated by you, the carrier. "Education" in this sense is enriching and broadening in areas you would not normally travel on your own—as to Ierapetra, in Crete. It is a beautiful scene that shows that Isabel Two has grown not only physically but also emotionally and psychologically. She is a "bigger" person on many levels. She can now be equal to Tristan. Beforehand, Tristan has thought of her as a little girl. Now he regards her with a new awareness.

Isabel Two gives him a puppy as her gift. We digress from the story here, because the puppy is an important symbol. The puppy raises the whole question of animals and their place in our lives. It is no accident that Native Americans are closely related to animals. That relationship is carried in their names, such as "Black Hawk Woman," or "The Bear Clan of the Hopi." Native Americans know the difference between grizzly bears and black bears. Locally, they know the plight of the Louisiana swamp black bear in the Atchafalaya basin and in the lowlands of the Louisiana sugar cane fields. Gratefully, there is now an effort underway to save this bear from extinction. There are license tags to remind us that the Louisiana black bear is becoming increasingly rare.

It is not surprising that American Taos Indians saw the bear in Jung as well. Here is a wonderful story told in *C.G. Jung Speaks* by Charles Baudouin.

> Jung had been living with a tribe of Pueblo Indians where, to identify a stranger, they do not ask for his passport, but instead they ask themselves, "What animal is this? Of what totem is he?" and they watch him, for to belong to a totem is to be the totem. So strong is the "participation," and the sacred animal has so impregnated the man, one has but to look at him walk and act and live to recognize him. When the man is from a neighboring tribe, the game is easy enough, apparently. But with a white man so different from all one knows, it is another matter. Jung knew, from his interpreter of his host's embarrassment at having failed to identify him. However, he had won their hearts sufficiently for

them to invite him one day—a sign of confidence and welcome—
to visit the upper story of the house. This meant climbing the
ladder. But while the Indians mount with their backs to the ladder
with the agility of monkeys, he naturally climbed in European
fashion, facing the ladder, setting his feet deliberately on the
rungs and presenting to the onlookers his square, powerful back.
A great clamor broke out then among the Indians, which he later
had explained to him. On seeing him mount that way, they had
recognized his totem: the bear! the bear!

Jung tells us that animals are often the symbolic carriers of our
instincts. They are the symbols in our dreams of the human condition.
What happens to animals therefore is literally a metaphor for what is
happening to us as a race of people, and as individuals. If we are
basically oblivious to the animals around us, then it is reasonable to
surmise that we could be oblivious to our instincts as well. There can
be a definite correlation between how we feel about animals and how
we feel about instincts. If we are unconscious of one, we are likely to
be unconscious of the other.

If you are familiar with Jung's life, you may recall that he had a
funny dog, a schnauzer that he brought to his consulting room. The
schnauzer had a great nose for psychotics, and one had to pass muster
with the schnauzer if he were going to be a patient of Jung's. In the
Remembering Jung series of videos, you may also remember Marie-
Louise von Franz walking her bulldog. Some of you may have read
Barbara Hannah's "Horse, Dog, and Cat" lectures. These are not
accidental. It acknowledges the close connection to the animal, to the
instincts, and to what Jung called "the symbolic life." It is not possible
to talk about the important symbol of animals if you have none in
your life. Dogs and cats are the two most common because they carry
the obvious instincts—the masculine and the feminine—right before
our eyes every day. If you want to see how the animal side of us lives,
just watch your animals. One can know a great deal about someone
psychologically by watching how he responds to animals. Classic
stories of cat people, and dog people, and the phobias people have
about animals can make it very clear that animals carry something
very important for human beings.

So again, a review of what our instincts are. Instincts are the primitive drives in us that are natural and vital to survival. They happen automatically. One does not have to think about them nor train them. They are completely natural to us. There are instincts for survival, and instincts for self-preservation. Instincts snarl when you smell a con. You know when your cat is hissing, or your dog is snarling, or your grizzly is about to lash out tooth and claw. To be conscious of those instincts is very helpful or indispensable for living in this jungle called modern life. The problem is that our instincts can be over-ridden by too much education and too much intellectualization. You can't intellectualize the cat in heat in your driveway attracting every tomcat in the whole neighborhood. You cannot intellectualize that. It is an experience.

We go into this a bit further. Education is good, but instincts can be over-ridden by too much education or intellectualization. That seems contradictory. Culture, or civilizing, can teach us to be social, to be socially pleasant, and to be socially accommodating at the expense of our grizzly or our dog (or whatever animal) which doesn't give a damn about it. When the grizzly or the dog doesn't want to socially adapt to a person, it won't. You can punish it, you can sit it in the corner until you are blue in the face, but it still won't like this person. It is a dog—it doesn't like this person, it doesn't like this person, it doesn't like this person.

You had better listen because your dog or your cat or your bear knows what it knows. That is the great thing about instincts. They know what they know.

You can override your bear, the instinct in us which can rage against the encroachment of our boundaries. If someone crosses our sense of what belongs to us and we get our toes stepped on—that is our bear. In fact, our boundaries are the great place in which to know about our instincts—to notice them and what shape they are in. In the book on typology written by von Franz and James Hillman, von Franz tells a great story about the Psychological Club in Zurich founded by Jung, and how each member behaved. Each would come to hear the lectures, and each had his certain seat—the place he liked to sit down in the room—and you had best not encroach, or he would growl and snap. Jung felt that the Club was a place that allowed the members to experience their instincts in a contained way, and he often learned what animal natures lurked inside his clients and friends. We do that all the time, only we don't call it that. Unfortunately we often do not notice. Instead, we repress all those reactions that are not courteous. We need to notice our inner animals. Some of us don't even know if they are alive. Chances are they are depressed, and in turn, they will make you depressed. Imagine a real, live grizzly bear—like the one in *Legends of the Fall*—walking around with us, all chained up, in New York City. It wouldn't do. Grizzlies are not meant to walk around on leashes or all chained up. It can be a dicey thing to have a grizzly on a leash walking down the street—your neighbors might not appreciate that. It makes people nervous. On the other hand, if you have the authority of your grizzly within, you can be pretty sure that no one is going to mess with you. That is the contained grizzly. People can smell him, and they will know that you mean business in a way that only a grizzly can mean business. No one messes with grizzly bears except idiots.

Learning to experience your instincts is a long, inner process.

First, you discover your inner animals, your dog, your cat, your bird—your eagle or your hawk—or your gopher or your mouse or your deer or your horse.

Second, you need to learn about it, and let it talk to you in your journal. Amplify it, walk around with it, discover what it likes and discover what it won't tolerate no matter how good a job you do in trying to convince it otherwise. That is the bottom line—*you need to learn what it will not tolerate*. You will learn that there are some things you do that it just cannot stand.

Third, and most important of all, you need to learn to trust its reaction.

A dog is a dog is a dog. A grizzly is a grizzly. They act according to their nature. Jung said that animals are the only creatures that never sinned. They cannot help but be what they are. Humans screw up all the time, which is the best reason for us to learn about our animals. We can trust them.

It takes work to learn how to respond to them. If an animal is sickly, you need to know how to comfort it and treat it. If it is depressed, you need to understand why. In the film, the bear— an animal essentially linked to the feminine—is central to Tristan's salvation. It gives him a great sense of being connected to another world, another reality. He is initiated into it. The bear makes him sensitive to the woods, and to the ride-off places in his life. He rides off, because the bear in him knows when it is time to hibernate. The bear knows about the rhythms of life. Tristan rides off. Finally, when the bear's voice has grown silent, he returns to the world. The chaos of Tristan's wildness has been related to, not killed, by hunting. His wildness has not been suppressed and overcome by willpower. Finally, Tristan has the bear, the bear does not have Tristan—there is a significant difference.

We began this series with Edinger's reflections about the fires of libido, the energy that must be transformed and made human. Tristan does that with the bear. He lets it be expressed. He has his inner bear energy now. It is carried inside. It is powerful. It is transformed, which means that it is integrated and harmonious with his ego. That is why the scene at the end of the movie—the final embrace of the bear—is so wonderful. It is the final "conjunctio." the coming together of the opposites. Many people did not like that scene. Some found it scary, or they felt it was a negative ending. However, that is an image of what Jung called "the final transformation." Here, at the moment of his death, Tristan is embraced by his wildness transformed and his wholeness is achieved. It is akin to the dream that Jung had before he died--that dream in which he experienced the completion of his life well lived. In Tristan's death, One Stab can say, almost triumphantly—although Indians do not talk in the same way as our "white man triumphant" talk—"It was a Good Death."

Isabel Two was also in touch with the animal nature. She connects Tristan to another important animal, the dog—the puppy she gives to him. Isabel Two plays a very important role in this story.

One Stab narrates: "It was then that Tristan came into the quiet heart of his life. The bear inside him was sleeping. It is hard to tell his happiness. Time goes by and we feel safe, too soon."

Here the film shows those wonderful scenes of Tristan and Isabel Two—the real connection, the real marriage. It is very different from his connection to Susannah, which was much more ethereal and airy and romantic. There is something very down to earth about Isabel Two and the connection between them. One Stab tells us that the bear inside Tristan was sleeping, that the wildness and the anger inside of him was integrated at last into the quiet center of his life. But just as we want to settle in, One Stab warns us against it: "It is hard to tell about happiness. Time goes by and we feel safe, too soon." So you know there is not "happily ever after," and the pain is not over. I am reminded of the words of Jesus, the great maestro of consciousness, who warns us, "Be alert, always." He said that just before the apostles fell asleep.

Always be alert. Not just most of the time, or not just when you have just overcome all the odds. Be alert always, especially when you are tempted to relax, when you feel happy, and when you are ready to let your guard down. Tristan is happy: then he lets his guard down, and a terrible thing happens as a result. The marriage suffers the same fate in the film that many marriages suffer—it goes the way of ricocheted bullets, ricocheted objects—those things that get people in the night, things that were not meant for them at all. When hearts and motives are not clear, other people get waylaid by our behavior, even killed by it. Therefore we need to remain alert because disaster always follows a letdown in consciousness.

We know that is disgusting and hard to take and that it goes against the grain. It kills the romantic myth. We can hear the romantics talking—"Damn it; can't we just have some fun? Can't we have a good time? Can't we have Mardi Gras all year round?" No. Mardi Gras is one day a year and one had better watch out even then, especially then. Disaster always follows a letdown in consciousness. That is an inescapable fact.

We see the disaster in the making, in the following scenes:
Alfred: Tristan's back.
Susannah: Yes, I know.
Alfred: [darkly] You know? How do you know?
Susannah: I saw him.
Alfred: He came here? Just to see you?
Susannah: No, he wanted to see you, but he thought you would get upset. I think he might be right.
Alfred: Uh. What did he say? What did—?
Susannah: He said to say hello and congratulations.
Alfred: Oh, silly me. So he told you the news, did he? Well what do you think? Come on—it's perfectly absurd, marrying Isabel Two. [Susannah did not know of this, but Alfred does not see her reaction.] She's practically our sister. She can't be more than

nineteen.
Susannah: Twenty. [Her face is turned away from Alfred, and he cannot see her pain.]
Alfred: You know I can't imagine what the hell Decker is thinking of to allow this.
Susannah: Well perhaps he is thinking of his daughter's happiness.
Alfred: Happiness? With Tristan? I think you of all people should know how impossible that is.
Susannah: Well, I'm not Isabel Two.

The acting is terrific in this scene, particularly when Susannah has her romantic dreams shattered. She writes to Tristan:

Dearest Tristan,
I was so pleased to hear of your coming marriage. Your father must be very happy. Isabel Two is like a daughter to him. She was named after your own mother. It seems as though it was always meant to be, doesn't it?

Isabel, Tristan's mother returns from the East, bringing the wedding dress for Isabel Two to wear. The wedding is followed by scenes of the two together, and fully available to each other.
The naming of the child. Tristan and Isabel's first child, a son:
Tristan: Samuel Decker Ludlow.
Susannah writes:
Dearest Tristan,
Alfred and I are delighted to hear of your son's birth. We had hoped for a child of our own, but hope of that has disappeared. I know Alfred thinks of you often. I look forward to the day when we all might see one another again. Your son bears a proud and noble name. I know he will live up to it. Please give my love to Isabel Two, to your father and everyone else.

Track 6, Alfred Moves

The music in this part of the film captures the feeling so well—it is fulfilling and ordinary and lovely. Tristan is back and he is in the quiet happy time of his life. Yet in the background is Susannah's face, along with her pain—her letters congratulating him in the face of her own disappointments, her own shattered romantic dreams. What did it mean that the mother, Isabel One, came back for the wedding, bringing the wedding dress, presumably her own? Psychologically, it could be that there was some healing of his mother complex. Tristan therefore is able to have a real life, with a real flesh and blood, down to earth concrete woman, with kids, and the puppy, the picnic, the second child, all telescoped as he rests with Isabel Two. Compare with that the horrible, increasingly dark other couple, Alfred and Susannah, who, literally and symbolically, can have no children. That contrast is played out perfectly in the scene of the meeting at the fair. Susannah and Alfred are there for a political speech, while Tristan, Isabel Two and their children have come simply to enjoy the fair. Susannah meets Samuel, Tristan's son:

Tristan: This is Sam.
Susannah: Hello, Sam.
Sam: [to Tristan] She's beautiful.
Susannah: How old are you? Let me see…
Alfred: Samuel.
Samuel: Hello. Who is this lady?
Susannah: I am your Aunt Susannah. I used to know your Uncle Samuel who died in the war. I think you look like him.
Samuel: That's what Grandpa says.
Susannah: He was very brave, very good.
Samuel: Grandpa says that too. Grandpa says I can have Uncle Samuel's gun when I'm bigger. Would you come and see it?
Susannah: I'd love to. Sometime.
Alfred: He's a fine boy, Tristan.
Tristan: He is.
Alfred: How's father? Is he well?
Tristan: As well as can be expected.
Susannah: I wish…
Man approaching: Pardon the intrusion. Excuse me, Alfred. I think we're ready for your speech now.
Alfred: All right.
Susannah: I'll be there in a minute. [Little Sam kisses her.] Thank you.

The shadows—the Irish politicians who back Alfred—are always able to break the tension.

Obviously, Tristan's complex about Samuel has healed. This scene shows the two ways of healing. The one who benefits is Tristan. He has named his son Samuel, his daughter, Isabel. His life is fulfilling and ordinary. The one who doesn't understand it is Susannah. She is increasingly pained and heavy and burdened. Susannah is so exquisitely in pain that it is almost hard to watch. The woman who betrays her heart suffers unbelievably. Susannah's face—as she talks to little Samuel—is really profound. Her face tells a story in itself.

The Irish bully breaks in. This is the Irish bootlegger, O'Banion, the supporter of Alfred, who is at the core of the destruction that follows. We talked about evil in people's lives and here is Alfred's evil again. He is indebted to the wrong crowd. Colonel Ludlow was right; for support, they intended to get their payment. O'Banion is a bully who thrives on guilt and intimidation, who tries to keep good people intimidated by subterfuge making them think they are guilty of misdeeds, when he is really the agent. In the film, his henchmen shadow Tristan, watching him. The "paid off police" intimidate and bully Tristan for his whiskey deliveries, but of course it is the O'Banion brothers who are the real profiteers of the illegal whiskey trade, and they resent Tristan's breaking in on their "turf."

You can see how their tactics work in the next scene, the terrible scene where Isabel Two is killed. This is such a terrible scene one would want to avoid it. We cannot.

[Tristan makes a delivery, and takes the payment in an envelope. Agents of the Irish mafia and the police are nearby, watching, with cases of whiskey in their own car. As soon as Tristan drives away, the police are told to get him. Tristan then is confronted by a roadblock as he heads back to the homestead.]

> Policeman: Sir, we have information that you are transporting goods in violation of the Volstead Act.
> Tristan: Well, if you mean a case of Irish whiskey for my father, I am.
> Policeman: I ask you to give it up.
> Tristan: He'll be a bit disappointed. [He then decides to resist.]

[The police fire automatic machine gun fire to warn him. One of the bullets ricochets off the stone of the roadside and kills Isabel.]

Tristan: No! No! NO!
[He attacks the policeman, and beats him, but is then himself beaten by the agents, while the Irish thug, John O'Banion, watches.]
Agent: Let's get out of here, John.
John: Get the envelope in his pocket.
[Takes the money Tristan has made for his delivery.]
Agent: [Insistently.] Now, John.
John: [To Tristan] My brother told you to stay out of our way.
[He hits Tristan with a shot-loaded club, knocking him unconscious. Then speaking to the agent, and motioning toward the policeman beaten by Tristan] Pick him up and load him in the car.

[Tristan regains consciousness, goes to the car, picks up Isabel Two, and carries her off into the woods with him, to be alone with her and his loss.]

As we have seen, the ricochets from the machine gun, the stray bullets, kill the woman. Those same ricochets occur when we do not accurately appraise the nature of evil. When we are inflated, we try to stand against evil by ourselves, with our own ego strength. The ego alone—especially without the grizzly—cannot withstand the immensity of evil.

Notice that One Stab said that the bear inside Tristan was asleep—he did not say the bear was dead. If you ever want to see a scene of justified grizzly, this is the scene.

However, the issue is a bit more complicated, because Tristan is in cahoots with his father over smuggling whiskey. He is allied against the bullies, the Irish mafia. One cannot stand against the shadow in righteousness or thinking, "my cause is just" or "we're on the right side, and you're on the wrong side." One cannot do that, because somebody is going to get killed, and in this instance, it is the innocent Isabel Two.

Marie-Louise von Franz makes no bones about this. She has commented many times about the innocence of Christians who think that they can get by solely with praying enough, by being good, and by keeping the rules. She says that doing that only invites the wolves. Well, here is a scene of the wolves, so visually revolting and repulsive, that it couldn't be presented any better. The moral of this story is that we cannot be naïve about evil. We have to be clear about our motives, especially when we think we are on the right side. If you think you are on the right side, you had best beware, because people will die because of you. Upon reflection, if we look behind us, we would see many people who have been hurt by us, or hurt by the bullets meant for us. That should give us pause.

Isabel Two died. That wasn't enough. Susannah died, also. Alfred writes to Tristan, "You have won her. I am bringing her home." Even in tragedy, he sees Tristan as his adversary. And it is there, at Susannah's grave, where Alfred confronts Tristan:

"I followed all the rules, Man's and God's. And you, you followed none of them. And they all loved you more. Samuel, Father, even my own wife. I would like a moment alone with her, Tristan."

Aidan Quinn looks like he literally lost twenty pounds for that scene—he is the perfect portrayal of the broken ego now. The rules did not work for him.

Moreover, Tristan also has questions. He says to his father: "I must be cursed by God for what I said after Samuel's death." But the father says, "No, Tristan. I will not stand for it. You have not been cursed." The Colonel stands up for his son, and so prepares the hero for the stand against evil to come. At the end, it is Alfred who shoots, and the thugs are all dead.

One Stab Narrates: "We buried the bodies, dumped the car in a deep pool in the upper Missouri I remembered from when I was a boy."

The jealous heart has healed in Alfred, the carrier of the darkness in the family. Alfred comes through. It is Alfred who has to kill the sheriff—the ambivalent sheriff who is supposed to be the upholder of the law and the rules—to forge the circle. Since it was his jealous ego which let loose the destructive powers, it is he who must bring them to an end. The sheriff—the one supposed to uphold the law—consistently looked aside while the law was broken. Bullied by the thugs, he must be killed because he is the symbol for all that has gone wrong in Alfred, the one who overlooks all that he has caused.

That is a wonderful reminder of our fragility, our frailty. We must repair the injury we have caused. We have to actively stop the destruction we have let loose. We cannot be like the Sheriff and just look away or pretend that the problem is over or behind us. One of the ways we can do that is through analysis, where we learn to get our hearts realigned, to get us back into our family again. That does not mean in our literal family—no. Indeed, many of us need to flee our families with all deliberate haste and speed. Our real family needs to be the family of those who consciously seek the Self, those who seek to get their hearts realigned. As Alfred had to do, we have to shoot the sheriff, the passive one, and the one who overlooks the shadow, or turns a blind eye. The shadow, in this case, is the Irish Mafia, the thugs, and the evildoer. The sheriff is the one whose right hand doesn't know what his left hand is doing. We have to know. We have to know. We can't be that kind of sheriff. We have to repudiate that ambivalent one in ourselves. If the hero is full of life, and is the rock that others break against, we have to have absolute clarity. We want to be on the side of the hero. Otherwise, we will break against the Self, and the Self will break us.

One Stab narrates: "Tristan lived to be an old man. I had been wrong about that. I was wrong about many things. It was those that loved him most that died young. He was a rock they broke themselves against. However much he tried to protect them. But he had his honor and a long life, and he saw his children grow and raise their own families."

7

Dealing with One's Bear

Track 11, Revenge;
Track 8, Tristan's Return

Over and over, we have talked about Tristan's relationship with his bear in the story. In Jungian terms, one might say Tristan works out his individuation through the bear. What does this mean analytically? How would one see this in a modern person in analysis?

First of all, there usually is the initiation experience or dream where the person encounters the animal. We saw that in Tristan's boyhood encounter with the bear.

Here is a typical beginning dream:

"I went out hunting for ducks and to my shock and surprise, I saw a bear in the distance, but looking right at me. I knew it was trouble. I immediately began to think how I might escape. So, I just took off running."

This dream of a client happened early in his inner work, and it was very clear how to his dream ego, the bear was the enemy, one to flee from. From his associations to the dream, this was true. Right away, the unconscious shows us this modern man's conflict with his own bear (since symbols in dreams always point to the dreamer.)

Animals usually point to instincts. And it was enough to know that this "very kind, good guy" dreamer was somewhere cut off from his animal instinctuality.

So far, so generic. Animal. Instinct. Dreamer=Animal=Instinct. But what about this specific animal, the bear? The dreamer associated big, ferocious and scary with this bear.

We know then, that somewhere he was cut off from his big ferocious energies and they scare the hell out of him. We know from mythology that the bear was associated with the feminine. We know that association from the Latin and Greek roots of the word "bear." Older religions associated the bear's positive motherly qualities (but not biological), with the ethical side of maternity, the side of motherly care and concern. The bear cub is born a shapeless, unstructured mass, blind and white and the size of a rat. Then the mother licks the cub incessantly and painstakingly until the beauty of its animal form emerges. Here, mother bears are more meticulous in their care than even human mothers.

The bear mother: endeavor for her young ones is her main characteristic. It is this infinite endeavor and loving care that are symbolized in the bears. (We might notice already the interesting parallel/conflict in Tristan who was broken from his human mother, and bonded to the bear mother.)

It is not surprising, too, that this dreamer had a huge mother conflict, both drawn to his "suffocating" real mother and a need "to get away" from her psychologically.

Very often this is the case where the human mother was not able—for a thousand reasons—to allow "the bear," the animal, to emerge in her son. It was quickly repressed into only good behavior. If the son did not have enough vitality to resist, grave repression would usually result. Often, in mid-life, the bear stirs within, demanding recognition from the dreamer.

Here is another dream, much later in his analysis:

"In this dream I am in the house where I grew up. As I look outside I see my mother in the yard near the house. Coming from farther back, I see wild animals, a wolf more or less leading the way and a bear near him with several other animals behind. I yell to my mother for her to run and I look for my rifle in case the animals are about to catch her and I need to shoot them. She makes it back to the house and I go on with what I was doing. Shortly after, my old boss is at the house to visit and I get dressed to go and see him."

In this dream it is very clear where this man's instinctuality is to be found: the house "where he grew up" or, "his mother's house." That is not where they belong: they belong with him, in his house, his psyche. The good news is: there are lots of animals and lots of instinctual energy there. But then comes the problem: it is either his mother or the animals, and he chose to shoot the animals (repress them again.) The dream ends ominously: "he goes on with what he was doing." That means, he forgets the issue, he forgets the animals, he goes on with life "as it is." Not a very good conclusion to this dream. He needed to work on the ending of his dream in active imagination, which he did. Sadly, the work was not strong enough to overcome his "going on with what he was doing."

There are also important distinctions made in connection with the bear in the hunting culture peoples and those of a planting culture. Joseph Campbell, in *The Masks of God,* presents this very well.

Bears are associated with the goddess Artemis, and while Artemis can be a ferocious nature goddess, she also is a sky goddess, even though living in wild places. So, too, bears. They live "in the woods." The primeval forest for us is where bears go, seeming to carry with them the secret of this form of initiation. Jung, with Carl Kerenyi, has an important section on bears in his *Essays on a Science of Mythology* (Princeton University Press, 1949.) Here Jung takes two dreams of modern people, and contrasts Artemis, "the active one" with Persephone, who "was completely passive...destined to a flower-like existence." In the first dream Artemis is the maternally, protective form of the goddess, protecting against the fear of the bear's wildness. (It is possible for the maternal to be actively positive; and often "wildness" is the fear.) Surely, too, Tristan's "wildness" was scary, even tragic, especially to Susannah. But, back to the goddesses: Persephone is the "patron saint" of hippie-types (and there are many of them, post "the Sixties"); Artemis is her opposite.

If our dreamer does not have a connection to the positive mother goddess, as here, he can be "lost" and have "to go riding off" for long periods of time until he is able to establish that connection. Often a real flesh and blood woman can help here, but she has to be stronger in her femininity than Susannah was. Susannah's psychic frailty prevented her from being able to be "the container" that Tristan needed during "his wild years." (And lest we get too romantic about relationships, it is important to remember here that it is primarily Tristan's responsibility to his bear, not his woman's responsibility. But having said that, a real woman can help, if she is strong enough in herself.)

In a sense, the Colonel in the film served the positive connection surprisingly. After all, it was his amazing love for Tristan that provided the rock solid ego Tristan would need to survive the storms and years ahead. Also, his positive connection was to One Stab, who serves as a "godfather" figure in the film (though not so much in the novella.) We mean "godfather" in the best and deepest sense here of mentor and connector to deeper things. Surely these two men exhibited striking maternal qualities as well, in their nourishing and supportive sides for Tristan.

Back to Artemis. She is not only a protector; she is also a threatening mother who in her temples demanded the great animal sacrifice.

In the second modern dream cited by Jung in *Essays*, he brings out this aspect of the goddess. This dream shows us the meaning that the initiate felt himself transformed into an animal and so underwent a sacrifice, but also a process of rejuvenation. By submitting to the death-dealing power of the goddess, he experienced rebirth as an animal. Brilliantly here, Dr. Joseph Henderson describes the result of this archetypal transformation *as the power to be*. It is certainly what Tristan/Brad Pitt carried. And it is that quality, this author thinks, that made the movie a breakthrough for Pitt, one that so many women were instinctively drawn to. Brad had that "animal magnetism" that transcends the screen. It is also why the author, Jim Harrison, carries such clout with so many men today. He seems to have that same quality that he imbued upon the Colonel, first, and then Tristan. The power to be. What a wonderful phrase. The power, the energy to live one's life. The courage and ferocity to meet enemies and overcome. The strength to overcome the downward pull of life when faced with it. The courage and resilience to pick oneself up when defeated and go on. The ability to look life's difficulties straight in the eye and not look away. We make jokes about it all the time, but there is great psychological truth in the humorous saying: "to maintain an erection symbolically." To maintain one's manhood in the face of putdowns, cutting remarks, physical defeats, and the taunts of a woman. Interestingly enough, a man's penis can literally be the indicator of what is going on within. Or as someone put it to me, "my penis often knows more about me than I do!"

Von Franz is positively brilliant in her *Puer Aeternus,* in her descriptions of the laming effects of a mother's worries and anxieties on her son's vitality and adventuresome spirit that wants "to go out and fight grizzlies, the more dangerous, the better" (and all the other "terrible" stunts of young men trying out their incipient manhood.) It can make a mother prematurely grey, and her best defense is to look away and let her own "One Stab" cheer him on. Anxious mothers can kill. (Fathers, also.) It may sound like an exaggeration, but it is a psychological fact too often ignored. Deep anxiety is not a "quick fix" or Prozac-amenable. It can be "cured" by a mother's deep work within herself and her descent to the goddess within. This, in turn, (as with Tristan but differently for a woman) will bring about a new feminine solidity that would make Artemis proud. For if there is one thing we can know about the bear goddess Artemis, it is that she certainly was not anxious.

The "power to be" is the same quality van Franz tries to invoke when she speaks of a man's *"élan vital"*—the "vital force" in a man (often associated with Bergsonian philosophy that was a combination of consciousness and nature) that we are talking about here. She illustrates this with the wonderful/terrible story of the great grey wolf that was captured in Alaska in the Ernest Thompson Seton Stories. This alpha male was a majestic creature but as he was tied up, he gradually died "as simply" as the élan vital drained away from him as a result of imprisonment. Here is her description:

> The result, as the zoologists put it, is that in the male, sex with aggression can be combined, but not sex and fear. In the female, sex and fear can be combined, but not aggression and sex. There you have the animus-anima problem in a nutshell. In other areas of nature, it has been discovered that if certain male animals lose their self-esteem, they die. There is a beautiful story by Ernest Thompson Seton of a particularly good leader and cattle-thief wolf in an unusually good pack of wolves. This leading wolf was caught with much difficulty and, being such a famous animal, was not killed but tied up and brought home. At first, it got absolutely wild, with wild, manic eyes, but all of a sudden, to his astonishment, Seton, who had the wolf on his horse and was watching him, saw that the animal's eyes became quite quiet and had a faraway look, and the animal relaxed. He was left tied up

in the courtyard, for no decision had been made as to what was to be done with him, and the Government had offered a tremendous price-but the next morning the wolf was dead for no apparent reason. It had died of humiliation, and that is something rather common, particularly in the case of male animals.

The same thing happens in primitive masculine societies. Statistics were compiled during World War II to discover whether primitive or more highly educated peoples stand imprisonment best. It was found that the more primitive the person, the greater the rate of suicide from despair. Apparently, among the most primitive people there were mass suicides; they just ran amok. In one American camp where there were well-treated Japanese prisoners, an enormous number committed suicide in an outburst of despair. It is also well known that primitive Africans cannot be imprisoned for more than three days. Bushmen, for instance, cannot be imprisoned, for no matter how well they are treated, they just fade away. They lose hope and die for psychological reasons. So it can be said that it is essential for the male human being to have a feeling of freedom and self-esteem and honor, and with that, a certain amount of aggressiveness and ability to defend himself. That belongs to the vitality of the male, and if the mother destroys that, then he falls an easy prey to the mother's animus. She punishes the son in a humiliating way, thus robbing him of his self-esteem.

Another very wicked way by which it can be done is through mockery. I know of a mother who completely lamed her son by her witty tongue. Every time he wanted to assert his masculinity and be enterprising, she would make a little mocking remark, which killed all his élan and made him look ridiculous. A young man who goes off to perform his heroic deed does appear ridiculous to the adult, but he should be respected, for it means the growth of masculinity. Boys playing at being gangsters and Indians are funny, but one should recognize the necessity for the assertion of self-esteem and feeling of freedom and independence. That is essential and stress should not be laid on what is ridiculous about it. For that reason, in many primitive male societies where they endeavor to keep their independence and masculinity, the women may not look when the males go around wearing animal masks and tails attached to their behinds. The women are kept out of most male initiations in primitive tribes, for they could so easily make a little mocking remark about the heroes, or something like that, and immediately they thing would fall flat. The men know very well that they look completely ridiculous in those demonstrative displays of masculinity and for that reason, they exclude the women. Women also have their mysteries, with the girl's first attempt at makeup and hairstyles, and the mockery by the brothers is terrible. They laugh at the way she has made her first shy effort at being a little feminine, so that usually girls prefer to get into groups at school and make their first attempts there. They are also ridiculous, so they hide from the boys. (von Franz, *Puer Aeternus,* pp 180-181, Sigo Press, 1970)

In fact, much of Van Franz' *Puer Aeternus* brings up the problem of instinctuality so that the wolf and the lion also often appear in modern dreams. Here is such a dream:

"I am walking in a dark alley and there appear Mafia-type Italian figures that are dark and threatening. But I have a lion with me, so it is scary what might happen..." The dreamer awakes in a sweat! Obviously this is a tension-laden situation, that portrays vividly and colorfully the gathering tension in his own outer life. The analyst's trenchant comment: "I wouldn't want to meet you in a dark alley."

This is the dream of an "outstanding" modern man, who was shocked that anyone would be afraid of him. Obviously he had no knowledge of his lion, much less of his Mafia-like shadows. He was going to be in for some "rude awakenings," as we say, as he gradually and painfully had to acknowledge and accept these terrible sides of himself.

But he has—and as in the temple sacrifices to Artemis, has emerged like Tristan, with those transformed, humanized energies now at the disposal of his ego. But that means, too, that the bear is not caged, nor the lion imprisoned. Which also can mean there will be "dicey days ahead" where everything is not pasteurized and homogenized. In the film, the Colonel gives a wonderful portrait of a man who has come to an acceptance within himself. Over and over again, he "shoots straight," cuts through things, doesn't allow his sons to B.S. themselves, and most remarkably, strips away every illusion they manage to present, as in Alfred's foolish power-drive to become a politician. Then, in that brilliant scene, the Colonel, old and feebled by a stroke, gingerly raises his shotgun and fires, killing the sheriff. He, who had gone "to the other side of the mountains" for peace, blasts away in a great bear-roar of justice.

Perhaps that is the precise "grit" that actor Jack Nicholson lamented did not come through enough in the film, "*Legends.*" Perhaps. Perhaps not. This author disagrees. The beauty of the film is a testimony to this wonderful "container" that managed to capture both sides. After all, the story is so terrible that too much "grit" may have made it more unbearable than it is.

While on the subject of the animal, we note a few personal reflections on Jim Harrison. He is physically as big as a bear. He literally lost an eye as a young boy that severely wounded him both physically and psychically (he speaks of this at length in his wonderful *Conversations with Jim Harrison,* University of Mississippi Press, 2002.) In the film when the Colonel has his stroke, Anthony Hopkins, with his afflicted eye, looks a lot like Jim Harrison in real life. Finally, Harrison is known to be "wild and crazy" as was Tristan. "Life imitating art"—or, more likely, as Jung has painstakingly tried to show, art essentially comes out of the psyche, the collective unconscious of its creator. As so, it reflects that psyche. In any case, Harrison reflects the wonderful energy of the bear—that wonderful enormous vitality of a living animal that fully has "its power to be."

It is such a peak experience when a modern man can participate in that vitality. This author believes that is the true secret of *Legends of the Fall* and that Brad Pitt and Anthony Hopkins carried it well.

Therapeutically, it is a vital issue for most modern men, especially those close to the unconscious, which includes most creative men. How is man to get free of "the devouring mother" so that he can experience "the freedom of the bear" without killing everyone in sight?

The conflict and the dilemma continue: how is one to balance those opposing forces without extinguishing any of them. (Cf too, von Franz' brilliant essay, " The Transformed Berserker" in *Archetypal Dimensions of the Psyche,* Shambala, 1999, pp 35-56.) She goes much deeper there, suggesting much inner work. Listen to her words: "Modern zoologists and countless psychologists these days are writing about the problem of aggression and the possibility of integrating it, abreacting it, or suppressing it. This shows how to really transform and integrate it. It is then no longer what we call aggression, but rather a clearly defined delineation and solidification of the individual who is steadfastly remaining "himself" without yielding to a group or falling prey to mass suggestion. In the many situations of collective panic that a nation can fall into, (author's note: think of 9/11) everything often depends on whether or not a few individuals are capable of keeping a clear head and not getting swept away by the prevailing delusive emotions." According to Jung, "This is the only way war can be avoided." (author's note: one wonders if the President's Cabinet is chosen for such men.)

One meets so many downtrodden and beleaguered men, good guys who mean well but who long ago have "lost their bear." All the Alfreds of the world, who try to "live by the rules" hoping that it will give them the bear. Certainly in these times of war-consciousness—with Afghanistan, Iraq, Bosnia and Liberia, and most of all, 9/11—we must know the difference. We must be careful about the bear of aggression; we certainly all need the Colonel's longing to "lose the madness."

Perhaps it explains the hunger for so many men's groups to try and find "the wild man" or to find their planet Mars, the fascination with the planet of aggression and vitality and sexuality being closest to the Earth, or the *Men are from Mars, Women are from Venus* fad, or the *Iron John* search seems to be part of that same hunger. This could be why the story is aptly called *"Legends."* If properly understood and experienced, it too, will be passed on as something not to be forgotten.

That scene of Tristan riding home with the herd of wild horses in tow symbolized that great transformation as we said earlier.

Here is a later dream of that same dreamer: "I went out of my house and I saw the bear. This time I was not afraid. So I went toward it, it looked at me, turned and went its way." Here in this dream, the bear is no longer the enemy to the ego. Rapprochement has been reached.

"The power to be" designates the initiate's ability to achieve the ego strength necessary to withstand the destructive onslaught of the collective unconscious on an infantile level. Separating himself from the wildness of the primitive mother by submitting to her rule, he nevertheless preserves some quality of his own wild nature, which is inherent in a man, but is always being eroded by the civilizing influence of the cultural mother. Somehow, again a modern man/person must undergo escaping from that mother. Henderson wisely points out that a modern child's use of the teddy bear, through whose mediation he preserves contact with the mothering instinct while separating himself from the real mother is a growing awareness of his instinctual, rather than obedient self. (Henderson, p. 23)

Also, in Jung's dream interpretation, there is the understanding of the dreamer needing to "descend" to the deepest level of his animal nature to acquire an ego strength that allows him to rise above—transcend—the animal level and experience a form of transpersonal awareness which cures these mother wounds from an earlier time. Alchemy speaks of the blackness turned to gold.

Now to the practical: how does one work with the bear?
- First of all, one must imagine bears in one's own imagination.
- Get to know about them.
- Read about them and follow your interests about them.
- Draw a picture of "your bear," not artistically, but simply. You should see it as a living being, alive and full of energy with the tremendous energy and power that a grizzly boar bear might have. Humungous! Ponder it. Watch it change.
- Try to imagine all that they might represent, without trying to "censor" anything out.
- Then, do active imagination with your bear. What does that mean? You must have a living dialogue with your inner bear, allowing it to speak to you (without interruptions) as if it were a real person closely connected to you. Jung considered that the active imagination was the most important "ethical" step in relating to the unconscious. ("It is what the ego does with dreams interpreted that matters.")

Hopefully and without reservation, this will begin a long inner dialogue where the ego, humbly and without reservations, allows the bear to speak its mind. This may be a slow process at first, for the ego resists, but gradually as it picks up speed (so does one's handwriting) the bear reveals itself more and more and you, the ego is influenced by it, willy-nilly. Of course, the more one does so actively, the more the bear begins "to have its life" in you. In doing so, the ego changes until gradually there is "the great embrace of the bear" dance, where there is really an interaction between the two. Of course, during this process one's analyst/therapist offers suggestions and guidance along the way. Here is how a patient of Jung's put the process: "Out of evil, much good has come to me. By keeping quiet, repressing nothing, remaining attentive and by accepting reality—taking things as they are and not as I want them to be-unusual knowledge has come to me as well as unusual powers, which as I could never have imagined before. I always thought that when we accepted things, they overpowered us in some way or other. This turns out not to be true at all, and it is only by accepting them that one can assume an attitude towards them. So now I intend to play the game of life, being receptive to whatever comes to me, good and bad, sun and shadow forever alternating, and, in this way also accepting my own nature with its positive and negative sides. Thus everything becomes more alive to me. What a fool I was! How I tried to force everything to go according to the way I thought it ought to!" (CS13 *Alchemical Studies*, p.70)

Tristan had angrily cut himself off from the Mother. Then at the end, she returns, carrying her own wedding gown for Tristan's wife. The circle was complete. This film is indeed an epic tale.

However, so too is the journey of each man who dares to confront his own bear along all the steps of his journey so that one day, they also can meet in the "grand conjunctio." Women have similar animal instincts and they need such initiation experiences where their experience of the Great Mother becomes meaningful as well.

The final embrace by the bear is the inspiring return of the hero, and the final *conjunctio* of opposites. We hope you feel the hope in this story because despite all the pain and despite all the terrible suffering, the hero gives us courage. For the Hopi, the bear is a symbol of courage and strength in the face of fear. The spirit bear is a symbol for all of us. It is a symbol of not only courage and not only strength, but specifically, and precisely, strength and courage in the face of fear. This film brought us a great adventure, and brought to us the distinctive message of the bear, which is to give us strength and courage in the face of fear.

Our hope is that you will imagine the hero, Tristan, in your psyche, and allow him to ride with you, bringing you home transformed—with the wild horses reined and running, with your hair flowing in the wind.

※ ※ ※ ※ ※ ※ ※ ※ ※

Special thanks to Joseph Henderson's *Threshold of Initiation,* "The Bear as Archetypal Image," p. 223-232

Postlude: A Tale of Two Colonels from "American Beauty" & "Legends of the Fall"

Track 13, The Legend

After working on *Opus One, American Beauty* and *Opus Two, Legends of the Fall,* it occurred to the author that both stories contained Colonels. Both were fathers. Both were war-related. Yet, both could not be further opposites from each other, much like the two astrological planets active at the time of writing, Jupiter and Saturn.

It seemed too much of a coincidence and challenge to pass up—and that it might be profitable to reflect on them both, as well as their opposition to each other.

First, their approaches to life: Colonel Ludlow seems from all accounts to have enjoyed life and had a great passion for it. Furthermore, he went out of his way—far out of his way—to find a beautiful place to live. That can say a great deal about a man, especially when it is the wide-open spaces of the West. Without going too far afield, it would seem easy to say that he had a great love for "spaciousness," with all that implies. He "allows" his wife to go East (even though the author Harrison points out that that was customary in those times.) He gives her space. In fact, one gets the sense from this Colonel that he is all about "space" in this sense. He gives space.

He gives great space to the Indians; in fact, he was so outraged by the American government's treatment of the Indians, that he left his post and the Army forever. He "adopted" One Stab, who not only lived with him, but also became his alter ego. His relationship with One Stab in the film is fascinating. Obviously One Stab is his equal, a confidante, yet one who becomes the mediator and narrator of the story, presumably because he is the one who read the "letters." In this sense, One Stab carries "the Self" in Jung's understanding.

But most of all, Ludlow is a man who knows how to be a man. Even though his wife basically left him (there are hints in the novel of a younger man), he in no way shows disturbance by this. And yet one has a sense throughout that he has a healthy relationship with the feminine, and with his own anima. Indeed, his letters reveal that. Jim Harrison points out that those letters really existed, in the sense that they were the letters of his wife's great-grandfather who rode with Custer and fought grizzlies in real life.

And even though Col. Ludlow lived way out in the wilderness, one had the sense he was truly at home, at least until Tristan went mad after Samuel's death in the war.

We now come to his relationship with his son. Even though one Stab tells us early on that Tristan is his father's favorite, it is clear that he tries very hard to be fair to all of his sons and one does not get the impression that his favoritism shows. After all, it is a dangerous thing for a parent to show favoritism among children. It is a failure of Eros of the worse kind, responsible for all sorts of family disasters, no matter how it is rationalized by the parent.

What we do know of Colonel Ludlow is that he is a man of honor—honor, not in the sense of Alfred's rules, but honor in the sense of defending principles, such as Tristan's relationship with Susannah.

But most important of all was his love for Tristan. It is the bedrock upon which Tristan's life flows. Even when he wanders off, he is able eventually to "come back" because of that rock-like connection to his Father, a father who was certainly very human, and unable to understand, yet could still be loving. So much so, that when he reads the letter from Tristan saying—"Susannah, I am dead"—the Colonel suffers a stroke and the whole homestead is bathed in grey depression. The beautiful place is no longer beautiful.

Those of you who have seen the film, *American Beauty* and read my *American Beauty, Opus One,* know that Colonel Frank Fitts, U.S. Marine Corps, played hard-edged by Chris Cooper, is an entirely different creature. Whereas Col. Ludlow achieved some measure of his own individuation, Colonel Fitts becomes identified with the shadow. He lives in repression, and thus is Ludlow's exact opposite. While Ludlow chooses life and its vitality, Fitts chooses repression, and wherever he goes, war becomes archetypally interjected and then projected on the environment. Because Col. Fitts is at war with himself, he becomes the archetypal symbol of the wrong kind of war: the war within oneself.

And then, of course, that war can so easily be projected outwards on everything he sees: his wife, his son, his gay neighbors, and especially the drug culture. He becomes the archetypal negative Marine: macho, rigid, judgmental and obsessed. In short, everything that can go wrong with a profession of war. In his war, there is no compassion: it is only "Kill the enemy!" And so he becomes the carrier of what Jung calls "the worse kind of evil"—what we do not see in ourselves, we righteously and arrogantly see in others. In fact, arrogance might be a good barometer of the repressed shadow.

It goes almost without saying that therefore he has no real relationship to his son. He is so obsessed with his son's drug use that he misses his own—the aphrodisiac of righteousness. He orders rule keeping (worse than Alfred in *Legends*) and he regularly "rants and raves" with all his repressed bear anger. For him, the bear is not faced, nor owned, much less accepted. No doubt, if we knew, he would be haunted by nightmares ripping up his insides, terrifying him. And tragically, as we see in the film, especially in the symbol of the Nazi Plate—a great symbol in the Nazis of a whole nation repressing feeling and the feeling function—and what terrible things are left in its wake. This happens when thinking is elevated to repress feeling; that was Germany under the fanatic Hitler.

These two remarkable films give us two dramatically different images of fathering. One who fosters love and endless waiting, long support, even in the darkest times, of his son. The other, a cauldron of unattended rage—the bear—exploding and growling for all to see until the father's ultimate homicide and suicide.

That is the choice: if we do not face our own inner enemies, those enemies eventually destroy us. (Colonel Fitts.) But if we do face them—even in the midst of great pain and suffering, (Col. Ludlow) —then, from the least expected place can still come a father's dream, in the redemptive "power to be" of an alienated son, restoring some measure of justice in a world gone mad with shadow-evil.

✾ ✾ ✾ ✾ ✾ ✾ ✾ ✾

Glossary

Alchemy
Medieval chemistry using symbolic language that Jung saw as precursor of modern transformation psychology. Used symbols that can be seen as stages in the inner journey.
1. They used the system of opposites that resulted in the forming of a raw substance.
2. Alchemy is a metaphor, which illuminates how a relationship with another person promotes internal growth and how intrapsychic processes promote personal relations.

Terms:
The Blackness
The hated thing in us.

The Tower
The place for the blackness to be transformed.

Conjunctio
Joining together of two opposites; marriage as a symbol of this.

Opus
The alchemical process and work

Prima Materia
The original material—usually dreaded.

Solutio
Solution. Where water symbols break down a hard mass.

Mortificatio
Suffering. Stage in the alchemical process where the elements are "dead."

(For a profound explanation as well as enumeration of symbols, see Edward Edinger's, *Anatomy of the Psyche* or Theodore Abt's *The Great Vision of Muhammad ibn Umail*, Supplement to Psychological Perspectives, Winter 2004.)

Analysis: A form of therapy specializing in bringing the unconscious into consciousness, primarily by work on one's dreams.

Anima
The inner feminine side of a man. Coming to terms with this is the masterpiece for a man. Man's work of individuation.

Animus
The inner masculine side of a woman. Coming to terms with this is the masterpiece for a woman.

Archetype
Psychic patterns of behavior.

Complex
A group of images or ideas held together by a common emotional tone. At the bottom of each complex lies an archetype or archetypal image.

Differentiation
The separation of parts from a whole.

Ego
The central complex of consciousness. The "I" we usually speak of.

Emotion
An involuntary reaction due to an active complex.

Epic:
Heroic, grand, majestic, imposing story dealing with events of legendary importance.

Eros
The function of relationships, relatedness.

Extraversion
A mode of psychological orientation where the movement of energy is toward the outer world, and/or the object.

Feeling
The function of valuing; the valuing function.

Feeling function
The function that evaluates what something is worth.

Hero
An archetypal motif based on overcoming obstacles and achieving certain goals.

Individuation
The word Jung used to describe the journey of an individual becoming his or her own unique self.

Instincts
An involuntary drive toward certain activities. Jung identified 5 prominent groups: creativity, reflection, activity, sexuality, and hunger.
  Creativity was for Jung in a class by itself. He also believed that true creativity could only be enhanced by the analytic process. Instinct and Archetype are a pair of opposites, inextricably linked and therefore you have to tell them apart.

Introversion
A mode of psychological orientation where the movement of energy is toward the inner world.

Legend
Something that is remembered, usually consciously.

Mother Complex
A group of feeling-toned ideas associated with the experience and image of mother.

Myth
An involuntary collective statement based on an unconscious psychic experience.

Numinous
Description of something that has a deep emotional impact.

Possession
State where a person identifies with an inner complex and loses his freedom of choice.

Projection
An automatic process where one sees one's own psyche in others or in things. It's "out there."

The Psyche
The totality of all psychological processes.

Puer Aeternus
Eternal child; someone who neurotically remains forever young. But can also be very creative.

Self
The Archetype of wholeness; a transpersonal power that transcends the Ego, the centering archetype.

Self-regulating Psyche
The concept based on the compensatory relationship between consciousness and unconsciousness.

Shadow
The hated sides of oneself which the ego represses.

Synchronicity
When an event in the outside world coincides meaningfully with a psychological state of mind.

Tower
The "secret" of alchemy; the place of transformation, especially of berserk bear energy. Jung's Bollingen is an example.

Trickster
Descriptive of unconscious Shadow tendencies. Also the one who is elusive and "plays tricks" on others; Hermes.

Bibliography

Abt, Theodore: *Knowledge for the Afterlife*, Living Human Heritage 2003

Progress without Loss of Soul; Daimon/Chiron Publications; 1989

The Secret Vision of Muhammad, ibn Umail, Supplement to Psychological Perspectives, Winter, 2003

Bedier, J., *The Romance of Tristan & Iseult;* New York: Vintage 1965.

Campbell, J., *Myths to Live By;* Bantam, 1972

Hero with a Thousand Faces; Princeton University Press, 1948

Masks of God; Penguin Books, 1991

Chachere, Richard, *American Beauty,* 2003; Cypremort Press

Audio Tape, Steinbeck's, *East of Eden*

Audio Tape, Van der Post, *The Hunter and the Whale*

Audio Tape, Van der Post, *Face Beside the Fire*

Audio Tape, M. Mitchell, *Gone with the Wind*

Video Tape, *Othello,* 2004

Craighead, Frank, *Track of the Grizzly;* Sierra Club Books

Eliade, Mircea, *Myths and Rituals of Initiation;* Spring Publications; 1994

Shamanism; Princeton University Press, 1972

Elsner, Thomas, *The Christian Archetype and the Nature Spirit,* 2003; Zurich: The vonFranz Center for Depth Psychology

Edinger, Edward, *Ego and Archetype;* Penguin Books, 1992

Anatomy of the Psyche; Open Court, 1986

The Eternal Drama, Shambala Publications, 2001

Archetype of the Apocalypse, Open Court, 1999

The Psyche on Stage, Inner City Books, 2000

The Mysterium Lectures, Inner City Books, 1995

The Creation of Consciousness; Inner City Books, 1984

Harrison, Jim, *Legends of the Fall,* Dell Publishing, 1989

The Raw and the Cooked, Grove/Atlantic, 2001

Conversations with Jim Harrison; University Press of Mississippi, 2002

Henderson, Joseph, *Shadow and Self;* Chiron Publications, 1990

Thresholds of Initiation; Wesleyan University Press, 1967

Henderson, Joseph & Sherwood, Dwayne, *Transformation of the Psyche;* Brunner-Routledge, 2003

Hillman, James, *Anima, An Anatomy;* Spring Publications, 1985

Hollis, James, *Swamplands of the Soul;* Inner City Books, 1996

Under Saturn's Shadow; Inner City Books, 1994

Tracking the Gods; Inner City Books, 1995

Johnson, R., *We;* Harper & Row, 1989

Jung, C.G., *Man and His Symbols;* Dell Publishing, 1968

Mysterium Conjunctionis; CW 14 Princeton, 2nd Ed., 1977

C.G. Jung Speaking; Princeton, 1986

Letters, Vol I and II; Princeton, 1984

The Spirit in Man, Art and Literature, CW15; Princeton, 1971

Psychology and Alchemy, CW12; Princeton, 1980

Alchemical Studies, CW 13; Princeton, 1968

The Symbolic Life, CW18, 1970; Princeton, 1977

Symbols of Transformation, CW 5; Princeton, 1956

Seminar on Dream Analysis; Princeton, 1984

Answer to Job, CW11; 2nd Ed. Princeton, 1969

The Archetypes of the Collective Unconscious; CW 9i; Princeton, 1968

Modern Man in Search of a Soul, Harper, 1933

Jung and Kerenyi, *Essays on a Science of Mythology;* Princeton, 1992

Lemle, Mickey, *Hasten Slowly,* Video, Lemle Pictures, 1996 (Life of Laurens Van der Post)

Lopez, B., *Of Wolves and Men;* Scribner. revised, 1979

Lorenz, Konrad, *King Solomon's Ring;* Signet Classics, 1982

Meier, C.A., *A Testament to the Wilderness;* Daimon, 1985

Momaday, N. Scott, *In the Bear's House;* St. Martin's Press, 1999

McNamee, Greg, Ed., *The Bearskin Quiver;* Daimon Press, 2002

McNamee, Thos., *The Grizzly Bear;* Knoff, 1984

Player, Ian, *Zulu Wilderness;* Fulcrum Publishing, 1988

deRougement, Denis, *Love in the Western World;* Harper, 1956

Russack, Neil, *Animal Guides,* Inner City Books, 2002

Ryley, Nancy, *The Forsaken Garden;* Quest Books, 1998

Sanford, John, *The Invisible Partners;* Paulist Press, 1984
King Saul, The Tragic Hero; Paulist Press, 1985
The Kingdom Within; Harper/San Francisco, 1987
Healing and Wholeness; Paulist Press, 1977
What Men are Like; Paulist Press, 1988

Sabini, M., Ed., *The Earth Has a Soul—Nature Writings of Jung,* North Atlantic Books, 2002

Seton, Ernest Thompson, *The Biography of a Grizzly;* University. of Nebraska Press, 1985

Sharp, Daryl, *The Jung Lexicon,* Inner City Books, 1991
The Secret Raven, Inner City Books, 1980
Digesting Jung, Inner City Books, 2001

Smith, Betty, *Loved by a god,* Audio by the author, 1995

Tacey, David, *Jung and the New Age;* Brunner-Routledge, 2001

Ulanov, Barry and Ann, *Cinderella and Her Sisters: The Envied and the Envying;* Westminster Press 1983

Van der Post, Laurens, *About Blady,* Harvest-Lightning Source, Inc. 1993
In *The Forgotten Garden,* Nancy Ryley
A Walk with a White Bushman; with Jean-Marc Pottiez W. Morrow, 1986
Venture to the Interior, Penguin, 1957
The Voice of the Thunder, Morrow, 1984

A Story Like the Wind, Morrow, 1972

The Hunter and the Whale, Penguin, 1967

Rock Rabbit and the Rainbow, in honor of L. Van der Post, Daimon, Verlag 1998

Video: *All Africa Within Us,* BBC, 1975

Von Franz, Marie Louise, *The Golden Ass of Apuleius;* Shambhala, 1993

Puer Aeternus; Inner City, 2nd Ed., 1981

Psychotherapy; Shambhala, 1992

The Feminine in Fairy Tales; Shambhala, 1972

Projection and Re-collection in Jungian Psychology; Open Court, 1985

Aurora Consurgens; Inner City, 2000

Archetypal Dimensions of the Psyche, Shambhala, 1999

Alchemy; Inner City, 1981

Shadow and Evil in Fairy Tales; Random House, 1995

Consciousness, Power and Sacrifice, Psychological Perspectives, Fall, 1987

The Way of the Dream, Windrose Films, Shambhala, 1994

Von Franz and Hillman, *Jung's Typology,* Spring Publications, 1971

Index

A

AA, 107
Abt, Theo; *Knowledge for the Afterlife,* Living Human Heritage, xvi
active imagination, 1, 142,
  long inner dialogue, 142
  practical work with the bear, 142-143
Actors: 107
  Anthony Hopkins: 3, 27, 140
  as soul man, 104
  as troubled, 104
  Brad Pitt: 3, 100, 104, 140
  Aidan Quinn: 3, 37, 66, 117, 131
  as broken ego: 109, 117, 131
  Julia Ormond: 3, 93
  Henry Thomas, 3, 21, 27
  Gordon Tootoosis, 3
Actor's looks: 30, 32
  Brad Pitt: 30, 32, 100, 104, 140
Aion of Aquarius: 81, 86
  Water Bearer, 81
Aion/Age of Pisces; 81

Afghanistan; 141
Bosnia; 141
Iraq, 141
Iran, 141
Liberia, 141
aggression; 6, 15, 33
  masculine: 33
  problem of: 141
Aikido, xxi
Alchemy; 16, 142
Alchemists; 16
Alchemical operations
  being broken, 16
  blackness turned to gold, 142
  Solutio, 49
Alcoholics; 107
Alfred: 28, 92ff
  as close to mother, 65, 85
  and Colonel, reunited, 77
  and Colonel over politics, 70, 71
  and Fall, 64
  and jealousy; 72-74, 92ff, 103
  and passion; 74
  as "keeping the rules," 103,

109, 131
  at Samuel's grave, 64
  painful scene, 65
  as the sober, responsible son, 29
  heroism, 66
  as hurt lover, 109
  as insecure, 109
  our Alfred, 109
  political cronies, 70
  secret love for Susannah, 72
  sin against the family, 73
  as wounded, 109
All Africa Within Us, xx, 64
American Beauty, 116, 145, 146
Amor and Psyche, (Robert Johnson); 54
Analysis: 84, 86, 101, 111, 115, 117, 133
  Initial dream, 133
Anger, 111-116
Anima; 42, 43, 47, 48
  classic anima type, 43
  Marilyn Monroe, 48
  Beatrice, 48
  Carmen, 48
  Cleopatra, 48
  man to anima, 41, 91
  negative, 116
  pure evil of, 116
Animals
  boundaries, 123
  dogs and cats, 122, 123
  grizzly, 112, 113, 123
  inner animals, 124
  as instincts, 119, 122-124
  as instincts in our dreams, 122
  intellectual experience, 123
  Jung's schnauzer, 122
  in our lives, 123
  Native Americans &

animals, 121
  symbolic life, 122
Animus; 43
  negative, 45, 101, 114
  pure evil of, 113
  woman to animus, 92
Aquarian Age, 81, 101
Archetypal, 59
  energies, 106
  transformation, 59, 100, 141, 143
Artemis, 135-136, 137, 139
Atkinson, William, Foreward, xvii-xxii
awareness; 58, 84, 142

B

Bear, 7, 12, 18, 22, 23, 62, 68, 74, 78, 83-86, 92, 99, 101, 103, 105, 107, 108, 110, 112, 113, 115, 117, 119, 121, 124, 125, 130, 134, 140-143
  as aggression, 7
  as Alchemist, 67
  as teacher, 103
  and astrology, 100
  Louisiana Black Bear, 121
  Ursa Major, 100
  Ursa Minor, 100
  as bear mother, 134
  in canyon scene, 130
  not dead, 117-130
  spirit bear, vi
bear as feminine side, 83
bear qualities, 85, 86, 87
berserk, 23, 83, 114
  final embrace, 78, 122, 143
  Jesus, 126
  going away, 67, 69
  Greek roots of, 83, 134
  grizzly bear, 83, 84
  healing dream of, 141

initiation by, 81-85
as lust, 6
as mother, 85
as Tristan's mother, 85
mother as afraid of bears, 84
not yet silent, 66
One Stab tells where bear is, 66
opening scene of a bear, 22
practical work with bear, 142
riding off, 64
bear's voice growling, 115
One Stab's description, 114, 115
The Grizzly, 115
healthy anger, 115
inappropriate anger, 116
"The bear's voice has grown silent," 74
sign of, 74
"to lose it," 20, 72
"to ride off," 72, 83, 84
Tristan's bear, 6, 66, 86
Beethoven, 31
Bernstein, 31
Blake, William, 31
Brünhilde, 47

C

Cain and Abel, 39
camaraderie, 26
Campbell, Joseph
  The Masks of God, 133
  The Hero with a Thousand Faces, 59
circle of completeness, 78, 79
Colonel Frank Fitts, 147
  as archetypal negative Marine, 147
  arrogance, 147
  as carrier of evil, 147
  at war with himself, 147
  identified with shadow, 147
  as not facing inner enemy, 147
  as obsessed with drugs, 147
  as repressed feeling, 147
  lives in repression, 147
  as symbolic of Nazi Germany, 147
  lives war, 147
Colonel Ludlow, 145
  and Alfred, 70
  Alfred & Colonel over politics, 70, 71
  clarity and experience, 29, 30, 51
  defending Tristan, 71
  and education, 97, 121
  ego strength, 29, 53, 69, 70, 136
  enjoyed life, 145
  loved graciousness, 145
  gives space, 145
  as father, 16, 27, 28, 29, 32
  as image of Self, 16
  shoots Irish man, 77
  Isabel's letter to the Colonel, 24, 25, 91
  knew how to be a man, 145
  letters, 87, 88, 91-92, 146
  love for Tristan, 133, 146
  man of honor, 146
  One Stab his equal, 146
  staying in touch with feminine side, 91
  as "straight-shooter," 50, 51, 53, 139
  stroke, 72
  and war, 7, 10, 16, 27, 145
  writings, 24, 52, 91
  writings to anima, 87, 92
  scene with Alfred's "bravado," 70-71
  scene with Alfred over

Susannah, 71-72
standing in the midst of pain, 69, 70
treatment of the Indians, 145
two Colonels as opposites, 145
complex, 111
Conrad's *Lord Jim,* xxii
confrontation, 110, 124
consciousness; xxiv, 22, 49, 56, 82, 123
Conjunctio, grand, 125, 143
container, 61, 82, 140
   for the psyche, 87, 88
   outer containers, 88
consequences, 129
Copenhagen (play), 10
Cornwall, England, 27, 59, 60
creative fire, 106
critics, 9

D
Dante, 43
death, a good death, xxii, 119,125
depression, 76, 118
   scene of, 118
discrimination, 20, 21, 22, 35
discriminating feelings, 20
Dionysus, 98
dreams: 119
   grey-haired men, 34
   healing dream of bear, 141
   hunting dreams, 133
   initial bear dream, 133
   lion dream, 139
   "mother's house" dream, 134
   One Stab's dream of Tristan, 118
   priest dream, 96
   reconciling dream, 141
   tornado dream, 119
   woman's heart dream, 41
drug culture, 16

E
East Coast, 26
Easter, 110
East of Eden, Jealousy of Esau cf. Chachere/Steinbeck
Edinger, Edward, 5, 6, 15, 16, 17, 18, 30, 125
   Anatomy of the Psyche, 17
   The Eternal Drama, 17, 18
   Transforming of the Libido, 16-17, 125
Education, 97, 121, 123
ego strength of Colonel, 29, 53, 69, 70, 136
Eliade, Mircea, 86
   Myths of Initiation, 114
   Shamanism, 86
élan vital, 137, 138
Elliot, T.S., *The Wasteland,* 86
energy; 16, 30, 31, 32, 78, 105-108,139
entheos, 28
enthusiasm, 28
epic, xxii,
Eros, 9, 13, 20, 22, 30, 42, 89, 90
   difference between Eros and narcissism 89
   Eros and feeling, 90, 91
   women and, 9, 13, 14-15
Eve, 5
evil, 63, 108
   getting over hurt feelings, 108
   hurt feelings as source of evil, 108
   nature of, 130

F

Fall, the, 3, 4, 5, 64, 109, 117
fathers and sons, 8, 19, 23, 34, 50
feelings, 1, 6, 13, 14, 21
  feeling function, 19, 22, 90
  "having feelings", 1
  "hurt" feelings, 106, 107
feeling side, 20, 21, 91, 92
feelings and valuing, 9, 10, 14, 22
feeling of awe, 2, 15
feminine, 121
  absence of feminine, 22, 47
  bear as feminine side, 83
  as receiving symbol, 35, 36
  honoring the feminine, 13
ferocious energies, 123, 124
France, 59
  and romance, 59
funeral rite, 63
  Tristan's funeral rite, 63
  looking evil in the face, 63
  dealing with evil, 63

G

Garden of Eden, 4, 5
Genesis, 39
going away, 67
  Tristan's going away, 68
  Tristan's leaving Susannah, 68-69
godfathers, 86
  One Stab as godfather, 86
Gray, Thomas, *Elegy in a Country Courtyard*, 88
Greek mythology, 98
Greeks, to play, 4

H

Hamlet, xix
Hannah, Barbara, *Horse, Dog & Cat* lecture, 122
hardening of the Self, 90
Harrison, Jim (author), 1, 26, 31, 87, 140
  Legends novella, 1, 87
  personal, 140
Henderson, Dr. Joseph, 86, 136
  Rites of Initiation, 86
  "power to be," 136-140
  anxious mothers, 137
Hemingway, Ernest, 19
Hero with a Thousand Faces, 59
Hillman, James, 42, 123
hippies, 135
Hollywood Stars, 31
Hopi Indians, vi, 96, 121
horrors of war, 62-64
humility, 107, 142

I

"idea," 28
individuation, 82
inner voices, 2, 30, 82
initiation by "the bear," 82-83
instincts, 13, 23, 81, 82, 120-124
  responding to, 124
intellectual experience, 123
intoxication and women, 48
Irish bootlegger, 129
  Bully, 129
  O'Banion brothers, 129
Irish Mafia, 130
Irish politicians, 128-130
  the shadow, 128-130
Isabel, the mother, 24, 26, 85, 127, 152
Isabel's letter to the Colonel, 24, 25
Isabel Two, 6, 69, 106, 120-125
  her death, 75, 129

as instinctive, 94
killed, 129; ricochet, 129
her knowledge, 94
puppy, 121
Isolde
   inconsolable one, 76, 118
"Iron John," 141

J
jealousy, 37, 54-58, 104, 108-110
   Alfred and, 37, 54, 73
   jealous heart healed, 131
   jealousy & laziness, 55
   as greedy libido, 56
Jekyll and Hyde, 10
Jerusalem, 110
Jesus and Mary, 17, 18, 35, 37, 126
Johnson, Robert, *We*, 98
journal, 87, 89, 116
   as written, 87
   containment through journal, 88
   giving form to the unconscious, 88
   pouch of letters, 87, 90
   as work of reflection, 89-90
Jung, Carl, xv, xvi, xvii, 5, 6, 7-11, 14, 18-21, 31, 32, 36, 39, 42, 48, 57, 62, 67, 72-74, 81, 82, 90, 93, 93, 102, 104, 106, 107, 111, 118, 120, 122, 123, 134-136, 138, 143
   as bear, 121
   and Kerenyi, *Essays on a Science of Mythology*, 115
   Pyschology and Literature, 106
Jung's Red Book, 106
Jupiter, 19

K
Koshare Kachina, 96
Knight, 59, 60, 62

L
legend, 1
Legends, film
   James Horner, musical score, 2, 15
   John Toll, photographer, 1
   Edward Zwick, director, 1, 15
   as beautiful, 40, 55
   as a container, 74
   as lonely-feeling, 72, 73
Lion, 139; lion dream, 139
the love problem, 35
letters, 12-13, 87
   pouch of letters, 87, 91
   Tristan's letter to Susannah, 71
   letter writing, 87-91
listening, active and passive, 1
"lose the madness," 10, 11, 40, 126
Louisiana, 121
Louisiana Black Bear, 121
Louisiana Swamplander, 121
love, 98, 110
   clarifying love, 98
   romantic, 98, 99
   romantic love, happily ever after, 98

M
man to anima, 40, 92
Mardi Gras, 126
Mary in the New Testament 106
masculine
   projection on women, 48, 49
   strength, 70

"Men from Mars," 141
Mother, 11
  absent mother, 12-13
  anxious mothers, 122, 137
  bear as mother, 85, 134,
  bear as Tristan's mother, 85,
    134
  Alfred as close to mother, 85
  conflict, 134
  Isabel, the mother, 12, 127
  "mother's house dream,"
    134
  mother's leaving, 22
  mother's return, 143
    positive, 124
  Tristan breaks with mother,
    85
  steps to, 12
musical score, 3, 15, 74, 120,
  127
Muslim, 110
myth, xxiv, xxv, 2, 4, 5, 59, 81,
  97
mythology, 97-98, 135

N
naïveté, 21
nature, 4, 5, 7
nature as healing, xx, 64
nature reversing herself, 118
Nietzsche (*Homer's Contest*),
  15, 33
Narcissus, 88
Narcissus Myth, 88-89, 99
Nicholson, Jack, 140
number symbolism, 13
numinous, 2, 15, 82

O
O'Reilly, Bill, 107
One Stab, 17
  as close to nature, 85,86
  as godfather, 86, 136

mentor, 2,3
  as narrator, 2, 3, 7
  as psychic connection, 86
  Self, 1, 145, 146
Orthodox, 110
"other side of the mountains,"
  10, 11, 40, 140
overwhelmed by the
  unconscious, 115, 116

P
Passover, 110
Persephone, 135
Pisces, 81
policeman, 129
pornography, 117
possession, xxiv, 114, 116-118
possessiveness and power drive,
  57
pouch of letters, 13, 87, 89,
  90, 91
"power to be," 140
Presley, Elvis, 106
promises, 29,69
priest dream, 96
projections: 5, 47, 49, 50, 51,
  55, 65, 82, 83, 93, 97, 100,
  115, 118, 147
psyche: 4, 5, 15, 16, 48, 81,
  82, 86, 94, 100, 119, 135
Psychological Club, 123
Psychology and Literature,
  CW v.14, 31
Psychological Perspectives, 58
puppy, 120, 121, 125

R
Rapunzel, 5
reactions, own, 13, 14, 45,
  55, 56
red-blooded men, 9
redemption, 59, 110
relationships, 98

working things out, 98
resentment, 108, 109
ricochet, log, 109, 129, 130
romance, 59, 60
   romantic tales, 60
romantic love, 98
   in the cemetery, 98, 100
Romeo & Juliet, 99

S

salmon eggs, 113
saloon scene, 113
   Mr. Sexton (bar keeper) 113
Samuel:
   betrayal of Susannah, 33
   death, 62
   letters to Susannah, 61
   as naïve one, 22
   sexual fears, 95
   song, 46, 47
   Tristan's reaction to Samuel's death, 63
   Tristan's reaction to God, 62
Sanford, Jack, *King Saul*, 115
   Healing and Wholeness, 55
Sante Fe, xviii
Saturn, 19, 103
   as taskmaster, 103
Self, 17, 40, 43, 90, 118, 132, 143, 146
Seton, Ernest Thompson, 137
sex appeal, 104
Shadow, 42, 44, 57, 128
   our shadow reactions, 44
Shamanism, 86
Shaw, George B., *Major Barbara*, 63
She, Robert Johnson, 54
Sheriff, 131, 132
Siegfried, 47
sons leave for war, 53
   ego strength of Colonel, 53
spirit bear, vi

Stalin, as freedom fighter, 11
"Stars," 17, 31
stiff upper lip, 69
Susannah, 27
   as anima woman, 42, 47, 48, 93, 111
   betrayal of her heart, 76, 93
   naïveté, 21
   at Samuel's grave, 64, 65
   Susannah's promise, 69
   psychic frailty, 69, 135
   her pain, 126, 127
   her honesty and courage, 65, 69
   her letters to Tristan, 127

T

Taos, Indians, 121
Taylor, Jack; story, 112
Tower of Babel, 39
transforming psychic energy, 16
   Edinger's quote, 16
transformation, 9, 61, 74, 78, 100, 101, 122, 134, 137, 139, 141
Transformation of Libido, Edinger, 5
transpersonal meaning, 30
Tristan: 59, 103
   and bartender, 113
   and his bear, 6, 11, 16, 68, 86, 103, 111, 142
   and his fate, 105
   and the calf, 110
   complex, 110, 125
   as father's son, 3
   and humor, 96
   the knight, 60
   myth, 60
   final encounter with the Bear, 78, 143
   going away, 69
   initiation, 23, 82

initiation experience, 82
and Isabel Two's sons, 128
Samuel Decker Ludlow,
127, 128
meeting at the fair, Susannah
& Alfred meet Tristan &
Isabel Two, 128
breaks with Mother, 85
leaving Susannah, 68
letter to Susannah, 71, 117
marriage to Isabel Two, 125
nightmare, 68
nightmare reaction, 68
reaction to God, 62
refusal of Susannah's
dreams, 68
return scene, 66, 74, 120
Bear, not yet silent, 66
and Susannah's re-meet, 75
as Trickster, 95, 96, 97
wild horses, 74
as wild one, 105
death, 125
Tristan & Isolde, 6, 27, 39, 60, 97-99
myth of romantic love, 6, 60, 98-100

U

Ulanov, Barry and Ann,
Cinderella and Her Sisters,
54-56
unconscious, 5, 11, 81-89, 99-100, 104, 106
overwhelmed by, 115, 116
the collective unconscious, 85-87, 104, 106
Ursa Major, 100
Ursa Minor, 100

V

Van der Post, Sir Laurens, 64, 100

Vision Seminars, 11, 90
Von Franz, 5, 10, 13, 35, 36,
41, 58, 106, 108, 111, 114,
122, 123, 127, 130, 134,
137, 139, 140
on hurt feelings as source of
evil, 108
*Archetypal Dimension of the
Psyche*, 140
The Feminine in Fairy Tales,
36, 108, 114
Individuation in Fairy Tales,
35
Psychological Perspectives
interview, 36
Puer Aeternus, 54, 139
Remembering Jung, video,
122
The Transformed Berserker,
140
The Way of the Dream, 4

W

Wagner's *Ring*, 7, 47
Wagner's Seigfried, 47
war, 7, 16, 54, 63, 64
war consciousness, 141
Afghanistan, 141
war paint, 87
We, Robert Johnson, 98
wild horses, 74
wolves, 137
alpha wolf, 137-138
woman to animus, 41-42, 92

Y

Yosemite, 112

Z

Zoologists, 137, 140

About the Author

Richard Chachere was born in Louisiana. After traversing the globe as a young man, he returned to Lafayette, LA, a unique area with a rich melting pot of French and Cajun cultures, and a smattering of Creole and Spanish Catholic traditions. The food is rich and there is music everywhere, spiced by a *joie de vivre* that brings life to even the most dismal swamp.

After high school studies in Illinois, Chachere attended Georgetown University in Washington, D.C. He accessed many seats of political power in the nation's capitol, and he personally met Presidents Kennedy, Johnson, and Nixon. During that time, he also made great use of the rich cultural scene of New York City, especially the art museums, Broadway and the musical theater.

He entered the seminary and studied in Rome, Italy during the four years of the 2nd Vatican Council where he was ordained priest in St. Peter's Basilica. He was an eyewitness to history-in-the-making—Pope John XXIII's "aggiornamento," "The opening of the windows"—and to the fall of the Berlin Wall. He later was a personal consultant to Josef Cardinal Suenens in Belgium, traveling extensively with him to many countries.

In 1978 Chachere began his practice in Jungian-oriented therapy, following his own work with John Sanford, Helen Luke and Morton Kelsey and leaving the priesthood. Shortly thereafter, he founded The Acadiana Friends of Jung, a lively center of analytical work and friendship where individuals go to find their own introverted centers. He has lectured extensively since that time and the themes of this work will soon find their way into print. His *Opus III, Gone With the Wind,* will be his next release.

A Licensed Professional Counselor, he lives with Susan Onebane O'Neal, his four cats, Ms. Kitty, Steiney, Ricketts, and Tet, and his two golden Retrievers, Sam and Susie.